Going to College with Autism

Going to College with Autism

Tips and Strategies from Successful Voices

Emily Rutherford, Jennifer Butcher, and Lori Hepburn

ROWMAN & LITTLEFIELD
Lanham • Boulder • New York • London

Published by Rowman & Littlefield
A wholly owned subsidiary of The Rowman & Littlefield Publishing Group, Inc.
4501 Forbes Boulevard, Suite 200, Lanham, Maryland 20706
www.rowman.com

Unit A, Whitacre Mews, 26-34 Stannary Street, London SE11 4AB

British Library Cataloguing in Publication Information Available

Library of Congress Cataloging-in-Publication Data

Names: Rutherford, Emily, 1979- author. | Butcher, Jennifer, 1962- author. | Hepburn, Lori, 1977-
author.
Title: Going to college with autism : tips and strategies from successful voices / Emily Rutherford,
Jennifer Butcher, and Lori Hepburn.
Description: Lanham, Maryland : Rowman & Littlefield Education, [2016] | Includes bibliographical
references.
Identifiers: LCCN 2016011964 (print) | LCCN 2016016152 (ebook) | ISBN 9781475826142 (cloth :
alk. paper) | ISBN 9781475826159 (pbk. : alk. paper) | ISBN 9781475826166 (electronic)
Subjects: LCSH: Autistic youth--Education (Higher) | College student orientation. | Autism spectrum
disorders--Treatment.
Classification: LCC LC4717 .R87 2016 (print) | LCC LC4717 (ebook) | DDC 378.0087--dc23
LC record available at https://lccn.loc.gov/2016011964

♾ ™ The paper used in this publication meets the minimum requirements of American
National Standard for Information Sciences Permanence of Paper for Printed Library
Materials, ANSI/NISO Z39.48-1992.

Printed in the United States of America

Contents

Foreword

At the age of eighteen, I found myself dreading the next major step in my life, my freshman year in college. While my feelings might have been similar to some of my peers, I had something unique about my experience that simply wasn't a factor for most of them. This challenging but special part of me was my diagnosis of Asperger Syndrome, now called Autism Spectrum Disorder.

I still remember vividly the day my mom and psychologist sat me down to explain to me what it was and how many of the challenges I had faced recently with my social, behavioral, and emotional skills were most likely a result of this diagnosis. While most people would have been confused, angry, or in denial, I in fact was overjoyed to finally have a name for it, and with that name, a better opportunity to get the help I needed.

I believe it was this embrace of my differences that helped pave the way for me to be successful later in life as an adult and a professional. Rather than being angry or resentful, my acceptance of the diagnosis became a beacon to light the way for my family and me to seek out help for any challenges I had, and it eventually led me to speak publicly about how it's affected me on a daily basis.

Although middle school was a challenge, high school, with a diagnosis in hand, was a much more positive experience in every way. Academics have never been an issue for me, but what high school did was reinforce the idea that parts of school could be fun, even if socially challenging. The best example of this is when I joined my first organization, the Minority Heritage Club, and I learned that there were many other people in my school that felt they were different, just like me, even if their differences were due to something other than disability, such as race, religion, or sexual orientation.

Starting as a member, I quickly rose through the ranks and eventually became vice president of the organization. In this capacity, my beliefs and assumptions about what it meant to be different were shattered and rebuilt through the amazing connections and friendships I made with the students and parents of the organization. In particular, I watched as one of our most beloved parent volunteers, Denise Buckles, battled a terrible disease known as Amyotrophic Lateral Sclerosis (ALS), or Lou Gehrig's disease.

This amazing woman and her courageous battle against ALS put my relatively minor challenges related to autism into perspective and made me realize that, as hard as things seemed, nothing was insurmountable, and I had no right to complain about my struggles. In fact, I should do what she did, fight and never give up. Unfortunately, Denise did ultimately lose her life to ALS, but not before we raised $25,000 for ALS research and saw her personal battle change our community for the better.

I firmly believe that the day Denise passed, she did so on her terms, when she was ready, and she never admitted defeat, something that I can't say for many people with and without disabilities. It is experiences like these that humbled me and led me to continue to remind myself that, like Denise and ALS, autism didn't own me, and as long as I believed in myself and asked for help, it never would.

As I continued my journey through high school, I made mistakes, but I also learned so much from them. For example, how insulting a teacher, even if you're right, doesn't help you get an "A," or how important it is to match the color of your shoes to the color of your belt. While these may seem like common sense to most, I can promise you that to me, they were not, and I had to learn each skill one at a time through trial and error.

It is so easy for educators and other professionals to forget that individuals with autism are very capable of learning, but we must be directly taught the skills needed to live independently and function in an increasingly social and interdependent world.

Graduation day felt like it would never come, and I was so happy to walk across the stage, not as a Special Education student, but as a high school senior with his friends. Interestingly, on my drive home from graduation, amid the rush of adrenaline, excitement, and relief was an impending sense of doom and fear for the uncertainty of the future. If high school was so challenging, how could I leave my parents' house, move an hour-and-a-half away, and attend a university of fifteen thousand students?

While the answer wasn't apparent at first, ten years later I can look back and tell you exactly how I got to where I am today, and it really comes down to three things: self-motivation, ambitious goals, and grit/resilience. With the support of my parents and mentors, I have always been motivated to achieve my goals. Sometimes it was to prove to myself that I could and sometimes it was to show other people that I could, but no matter the reason, I will never underestimate the power of motivation to change the lives of my students or clients.

Secondly, ambitious goals have served as my road map throughout my college and career experiences to remind me what I am working for. Sometimes they were written, sometimes they were not, but they were always effective at helping me see the "why" in life. Lastly, the idea of grit/resilience is something new that I have come to understand has been the key factor in my decision to continue past any obstacles I've ran into and succeed while others with my diagnosis have failed and been unable to pick themselves up and continue.

Some people may equate grit with being physically tough, but it is so much more than that. To me, grit is facing obstacle after obstacle, tripping, falling, and failing, yet picking yourself up over and over again and repeating, "I will let nothing and no one stop me from reaching my potential and achieving my goals."

As a professional and an adult with autism, I am very proud of what I and many other adults with autism have accomplished, but I am even more eager to witness how we will change our lives and the world in the future. With this vision, my hope is that this book and its contents will serve as a catalyst for everyone to believe in and support the tremendous college potential of students with autism.

—James Williams

Preface

Have patience with all things, but chiefly have patience with yourself. Do not lose courage in considering your own imperfections, but instantly set about remedying them—every day begin the task anew.

—Francis de Sales

Students with disabilities are enrolling in college programs at an all-time high. Subsequently, higher-education institutions are faced with the unique challenges of meeting the needs of these students, particularly the needs of students with autism. Students with disabilities need to know their rights and responsibilities prior to starting their postsecondary journey.

There is a current push in special education, both at the national and state level, to provide appropriate transition planning for individuals with disabilities, particularly those with autism. Multiple states are requiring school districts to identify a transition designee for the district. Hong, Haefner, and Slekar (2011) noted that students who are successful in college know who they are, what they want, their areas of strength and weakness, and how to reach their goals.

As professors of education and former teachers and administrators, we know the impact of meeting the needs of students, particularly those with disabilities. Hughes (2009) reported that the most common accommodations, which are provided to students with disabilities, are additional time on exams, mentors/tutors, and alternative exam locations. Yet Hughes argued that institutions could provide more accommodations that would benefit students.

We have observed the struggles our colleagues have while working with students with autism in their classrooms. We have been told many times that they are simply not prepared to meet the unique needs of these individual students. There is a need for training and support in the university classrooms. We believe that with the right supports, students with autism can be successful in college.

This book provides students and professionals in higher education with information to better support individuals with autism. The intended readership for this book includes educators and students in secondary and higher education, high school counselors, and high school transition specialists.

The text presents information in a well-defined, succinct, and inspiring manner. Each chapter follows the same format. They are designed to provide readers with the latest information on each topic discussed as well as suggestions for ways to assist students in the classroom.

Chapter Highlights are included to provide an easy reference at the end of each chapter. The Ponder and Wonder segment explores possible discussion questions to be used in conjunction with the book. The last section in each chapter, Voices of Success, gives direct quotes from students with autism, detailing their personal stories of success in college. Finally, there are resources that will prove to be useful for both students and faculty along with Weblinks that can be used as both a guide and a point of reference.

Acknowledgments

The original idea for this book derived from the findings of our research involving college students with Autism Spectrum Disorders. We acknowledge the students who willingly shared their Voices of Success. It is through their experiences that a path has been laid to allow others to follow in their footsteps toward success in higher education.

Thank you to our families for their faithful support of our work and always allowing us to chase our dreams. A special thanks goes to Leslie Underwood for her countless hours spent helping us with editing. Thank you, Tanya Thompson, for edits as well. We want to thank James Williams for sharing his story in the forward to this text. We would also like to thank the scholars who served as reviewers and provided their endorsements for the book.

This book could not have been written without the support from our friends and colleagues who willingly listened to our ideas and unwaveringly answered all of our questions. We offer a special thanks to Dr. Sandra Harris for her mentoring and encouragement throughout this process.

Finally, with deep appreciation, we acknowledge Dr. Tom Koerner, vice president and publisher for education issues at Rowman & Littlefield Publishing Group, for his patience and guidance. He provided us support in each step of this process.

Introduction

Many college campuses are diligently working to improve programming for students with autism on their campuses. Increasing enrollment and demands often leave college professionals with questions about the best ways to support these students. Having a clear understanding of autism and ways to assist those with autism can maximize the college experience for both students and college professionals. This book is geared toward college professionals but also provides valuable information to secondary school special educators, families, friends, and students.

Chapter 1 gives a glimpse into how students with Autism Spectrum Disorder (ASD) function on college campuses by defining autism, discussing the prevalence of ASD, and identifying the common characteristics of students with ASD. Chapter 2 covers common learning differences that college professors and staff may encounter while working with students with ASD. The chapter mentions behavioral differences students with ASD may have that are often puzzling to others. Chapter 3 focuses on self-determination. Information is provided for teaching students with ASD self-determination at home and at school.

In chapter 4, transition planning is discussed. The importance of setting goals is explored as well as the importance of collaboration. The chapter also includes information that explains what the end of entitlement means for students with ASD, and it provides links to agencies that can help students make the transition to postsecondary education.

Chapter 5 explores communication challenges with professors, campus personnel, and peers. Strategies for ease of communication are detailed as well. Chapter 6 focuses on time management. The importance of course management, scheduling, and organizational skills are presented in a manner that students and college professionals may implement easily.

Chapter 7 gives information on developing relationships. Chapter 8 focuses on personal independence, which includes parents' roles in helping their children develop the skills needed to be as independent as possible.

Chapter 9 provides strategies for success. It expounds upon the importance of individuals having knowledge about their disability and how it affects them, the importance of students knowing what support systems are available, and the importance of students knowing what works best for them. Finally, chapter 10 includes concise details regarding college preparation.

At the end of each chapter, stories of success are shared with the reader. All of the voices shared are real-life stories from college students with autism. These voices provide readers with a rare and unique perspective of what it is like to be a college student with autism.

Chapter One

Defining Autism

Shattuck et al. (2012) found in their study that comparing individuals with learning disabilities and individuals with speech/language impairment, individuals with Autism Spectrum Disorder (ASD) were enrolled in postsecondary education at a lower rate than the aforementioned groups. The researchers concluded that the only group that was less likely to be enrolled in postsecondary education was those with intellectual disabilities.

Taylor and Seltzer (2011) indicated that nearly 50 percent of the participants who did not have a comorbid diagnosis of intellectual disability (ID) were pursuing some type of postsecondary education. They confirmed that postsecondary education is an attainable option for individuals with ASD, if they do not have a second diagnosis of ID.

Chiang, Cheung, Hickson, Xiang, and Tsai (2012) used National Longitudinal Transition Study-2 (NLTS2) data to discover that 43 percent of those with ASD participated in postsecondary education. Postsecondary education is a viable option for many individuals with ASD, but there should be a great deal of planning and support to aid the student (Roberts, 2010). This chapter attempts to give a glimpse into how students with ASD function on college campuses by defining autism, discussing the prevalence of ASD, and identifying the common characteristics of students with ASD.

Russell, a twenty-one-year-old male diagnosed with High-Functioning Autism who is currently in his third year at a technical community college, emphasized the following:

> A lot of teachers don't understand autism; it's not psychological. It's a neurological disorder, it's like almost like developmental issues, it's not retardation; it's not schizophrenia. For example, I can't really pigeonhole this subject. I can't really put it in a medical dictionary.

I don't really know the symptoms, but I have hypersensitive hearing, taste, smell, and it really affected me a lot back when I was a little kid. I noticed that there is really no specific pattern. You can't really pinpoint what is going to happen, and the symptoms are very versatile.

AUTISM SPECTRUM DISORDERS

The definition of ASD has been a topic of debate since 1944 when the world was first introduced to Asperger Syndrome by Hans Asperger. While many researchers feel that the differentiated definitions of ASD are not necessary, others find the differentiated definitions useful. In this section, ASD is explored with past and present definitions.

PAST DEFINITION OF ASD

Autism Spectrum Disorders (ASD) is defined as a group of pervasive, developmental disabilities that cause significant social, communication, and behavioral challenges and that manifest before the age of three. ASDs are spectrum disorders that affect each person in different ways and can range from very mild to severe. There are three different types of ASDs: Autistic Disorder, Asperger Syndrome (AS), and Pervasive Developmental Disorder-Not Otherwise Specified (PDD-NOS).

Autistic Disorder

Significant language delays, social challenges, communication challenges, unusual behaviors, unusual interests, and intellectual impairment characterize Autistic Disorder. This term is also called *classic autism* and is what most people think of when hearing the term *autism* (American Psychiatric Association [APA], 2013; Centers for Disease Control and Prevention [CDC], 2012).

Asperger Syndrome (AS)

AS is a diagnosis given to individuals with higher-functioning autism who do not display clinically significant delays in expressive or receptive language or cognitive development. These individuals typically present with restricted interests or repetitive and stereotyped patterns of behavior, abnormalities in reciprocal social interaction common to individuals diagnosed with autism (American Psychiatric Association [APA], 1994).

Pervasive Developmental Disorder-Not Otherwise Specified (PDD-NOS)

PDD-NOS is characterized by severe and persistent impairment in the areas of social relations and communication. Individuals may meet some of the criteria for Autistic Disorder or Asperger Syndrome but not all, or have fewer or milder symptoms and a later age of onset than those with autistic disorder (CDC, 2012; APA, 1994).

HIGH-FUNCTIONING AUTISM (HFA)

HFA is a diagnosis given to individuals considered to be on the autism spectrum who have developed language and function with average to above-average intelligence or cognitive abilities (Lane & Kelly, 2012). According to Fombonne (2003), a Swiss psychologist named Eugen Bleuler originally coined the term *autism* as a sign of schizophrenia. Lyons and Fitzgerald (2007) reported that Leo Kanner, who is considered to be the pioneer of autism research, published his first paper on autism in 1943. A year later, in 1944, Hans Asperger published his paper on autism.

Autism was not included in the American Psychiatric Association's (APA) *Diagnostic and Statistical Manual of Mental Disorders* (DSM) until its third published version in 1980. In the DSM-III, it was referred to as "infantile autism," and was identified as not being child schizophrenia (APA, 1980). Hart and Brehm (2013) noted that autism was included in the 1990 version of the Individuals with Disabilities Education Act (IDEA). Prior to that, Cohen (2011) reported that individuals were identified as being emotionally disturbed or as having a learning disability.

In 1994, the fourth edition of the DSM was published, and according to Grzadzinski, Huerta, and Lord (2013), autism was then a "multi-categorical system of diagnosing pervasive developmental disorders [PDDs]" (p. 1). The categories included: Autistic Disorder, Asperger Syndrome, Pervasive Developmental Disorder-Not Otherwise Specified, Childhood Disintegrative Disorder, and Rett Syndrome.

MODIFICATIONS TO THE DEFINITION

In 2013, when the fifth edition of the DSM was published, Grzadzinski, Huerta, and Lord (2013) reported that the multicategorical system had been replaced with a single diagnosis of Autism Spectrum Disorder (ASD). Savoy (2014) clarified that a common misconception since the publication of the DSM-5 is that autism is a single condition, when in fact it is an "umbrella term" that includes each of the categories that were listed in the DSM-4.

According to the DSM-5 (2013), ASD is diagnosed by significant deficits in social communication, social interactions, and repetitive patterns of behavior. Ackles, Fields, and Skinner (2013) reported that ASD affects each individual differently, and symptoms can range from mild to severe, which is where the term *spectrum* has derived. Dente and Coles (2012) also stressed that knowing one person with ASD does not mean that one understands all individuals with ASD because it affects every individual differently.

PREVALENCE

The number of individuals being diagnosed with an Autism Spectrum Disorder is on the rise. In 2014, the Center for Disease Control (CDC) released the latest figures as 1 in 68 being diagnosed. In 2012, the CDC reported 1 in 88 individuals was diagnosed with an Autism Spectrum Disorder, and in 2000, 1 in 150 individuals was diagnosed.

There are several reasons as to why there has been such an increase in identification. First of all, the medical community knows more about autism and how to identify it. Also, the diagnostic criteria changed with the publication of the DSM-5 (2013) when the multicategorical system was eliminated and ASD became an "umbrella term" that encompassed the five former categories: Autistic Disorder, AS, PDD-NOS, Childhood Disintegrative Disorder, and Rett Syndrome. Finally, there are better diagnostic tools available to professionals for the identification of ASD. These are just a few of the proposed reasons for the increase.

Autism does not discriminate, and it affects all races and ethnicities, sexes, socioeconomic status, and geographic regions. Boys are five times more likely to be diagnosed than girls. There are theories as to why males were identified at a higher rate, but they are only theories. Also, girls are often misdiagnosed with Attention Deficit Disorder, depression, anxiety, or obsessive-compulsive disorder. There is also growing evidence that females who were misdiagnosed are being correctly diagnosed later in life.

Families who have a child with ASD have an increased chance of having a second child with ASD. According to the CDC (2014), there is a 2 to 18 percent chance of a second child having ASD. Children born to older parents are also considered more at risk for ASD.

PREVALENCE IN HIGHER EDUCATION

As the number of individuals being identified with ASD increases, there is also an increase in the number of those individuals going into higher education. In 2015, researchers from the A. J. Drexel Autism Institute released their National Autism Indicators Report. In that report, it was declared that fifty thousand students with autism leave high school each year, and of those young adults, only 36 percent enroll in postsecondary education, which is far lower than peers with other disabilities such as speech-language impairment or a specific learning disability.

For those students who go into postsecondary education, only approximately 40 percent of those students disclosed their disability to their institution of higher education and received any accommodations or help. When students leave high school, they are no longer entitled to services that they received in public education.

In order to receive any services in postsecondary education, students must seek out services and disclose their disability to their school. They must be willing to advocate for themselves so they can receive services, and this is often a new role for these students. Due to this, it is difficult to gain a true number of students with ASD who are enrolled in postsecondary education, as many of them do not disclose their disability.

Students who did disclose their disability were able to receive these types of available services: testing accommodations, human aides, assignment accommodations, materials/technical adaptations, and physical adaptations. Students with ASD need support to be successful in postsecondary education, and their services must be individualized based on the needs of the student. To know one individual with ASD means you only know that person. Each person is different, and they have their own set of strengths and weaknesses.

CHARACTERISTICS OF COLLEGE STUDENTS WITH AUTISM

An increase in the diagnosis of individuals with ASD can be linked to an increase in the number of individuals with autism attending college. While students with ASD have been attending college for years, the increased focus on transition planning allows it to be more common for professors to encounter these students in their classrooms.

Many of these individuals are excellent students and require minimum support from their professors; however, there are some students with ASD who provide challenges for even the most seasoned professors. Students with ASD often struggle with communication, social relations, restricted activities or interests, and sensory processing. When professors do not understand the struggles of these students, they, like their students, can find themselves both frustrated and perplexed.

COMMUNICATION

Students with ASD grapple with many aspects of communication. Lack of eye contact is a common characteristic that is often confused with a lack of engagement, interest, and boredom. This lack of eye contact may appear disrespectful to others when the nature of looking someone in the eyes is simply an anxiety-inducing activity for these students. Most college students with ASD will have adequate expressive language skills but will struggle with the reciprocity, or the give and take, aspects of conversations.

This may lead to others feeling as if these students are rude and only interested in what they want to talk about. They may not understand pragmatic rules of communicating with others. Pragmatics includes both comprehension and production of speech sounds. According to Wolf, Brown, Bork, Volkmar, and Klin (2009), this could possibly be the most hindering characteristic for individuals with ASD because it oftentimes leads to isolation, low self-esteem, and sometimes depression.

Comprehension of spoken language can prove to be especially difficult for these students. They are oftentimes oblivious to the meaning of sarcasm and figurative language. This will lead to others feeling as though the students have lost the essence of the conversation and they grow bored of trying to communicate with them.

A less common characteristic of college students with autism may be that they have a difficult time processing language when background noise is prominent. This may occur in social situations (bars, parties, dorm meetings) or in noisy classrooms, and may cause them to completely avoid these situations; or in noisy classroom situations, they may avoid communicating with others because they really do not understand what is going on.

SOCIAL RELATIONS

Social impairments can be one of the most hindering aspects of the disability for many students. Individuals with ASD often struggle with making and maintaining eye contact, initiating conversations, and respecting others' personal space. Verbal and nonverbal cues are difficult for these students to decipher. They also struggle with the understanding of figurative language and the humor that goes along with it.

Students with ASD long for friendships and relationships; however, they do not know how to interact in a manner that would facilitate the development of these relationships. These students are often described as "socially awkward." They may seem uninterested in what others have to say to them or may even perseverate on topics they find interesting. Students with ASD also have a difficult time with the hierarchical rules of socially interacting with friends and family versus professors and employers.

RESTRICTED INTERESTS AND REPETITIVE BEHAVIORS

Individuals with ASD display restricted interests and repetitive behaviors. They will often have an unusual preoccupation of certain objects, topics, or ideas. They may only be interested in doing a restricted activity and totally exclude other activities or areas of interests. For example, an area of special interest may be cats. The student will only be interested in talking about cats or doing activities that involve cats. The student with ASD will often dominate all conversations and collaborations with lengthy, detailed information on their restricted topic, causing others to become uninterested and weary of initiating conversations with the student.

College students with ASD may also engage in repetitive behaviors such as hand flapping, pacing, making humming sounds, and the uncontrollable need to fidget. These behaviors are often stress induced and feel uncontrollable to the student. Others may perceive this as odd behavior, and it sometimes can cause others to feel fear because they are not familiar with the purpose and meaning of these behaviors.

SENSORY PROCESSING

Sensory issues are common among these students. They may have dysfunctions in the processing of sensory information, which can cause them to have adverse reactions to sights, sounds, smells, and tastes. For example, they may have an adverse reaction to perfume that smells very nice to the rest of us, or they may have a difficult time with the feeling of the tags or seams of their clothing.

The sounds of LED lights, air conditioners, and fans can be extremely frustrating, even painful, to these students. These sensory outputs can seem exaggerated and even disgusting to the student due to their extreme sensitivity and inability to properly process the sensory stimulation.

CHAPTER HIGHLIGHTS

- In order for students with ASD to receive services in higher education, they must seek out those services and disclose their disability.
- ASD affects each individual differently, and symptoms can range from mild to severe, which is where the term *spectrum* has derived.

- Students with ASD often display unconventional behaviors due to issues with communication, social relations, restricted activities or interests, and sensory processing.

PONDER AND WONDER

1. What are your thoughts on modifying the definition for ASD?
2. Have you seen an increase in students with ASD on your campus?
3. What characteristics have you found particularly challenging to deal with in your classroom?

VOICES OF SUCCESS

Paris is a twenty-three-year-old female diagnosed with Asperger Syndrome who is currently in medical school. The conversation began by asking Paris about the history of her diagnosis and her educational journey. She gladly shared her story:

> I was twenty-two when I was diagnosed with Asperger's. I always kind of felt like I was on a different planet. When I was a small child, I was kind of wired differently somehow. It never really tripped me out. I am in medical school and we studied Asperger's in school. The light bulb just went on and I was like, "Oh my God!" This is my entire existence in a nutshell. That was kind of a light bulb moment for me. My diagnosis has definitely helped me.

Jimmy was diagnosed with Asperger Syndrome when he was twelve. He recalled how he was told about his diagnosis:

> I went to a psychologist, and he interviewed my mom and I separately, and then after he did that, I didn't know what he was doing at the time, but now I know he did the GADS, the Gilliam Asperger's Disorder Scale, and the percentage was really high. It was like upper 90s. So then he called my mom and I in, and he explained it to her first without me, and then they called me, and then he actually told me, and my mom was with me.

Jimmy recalled, "After the diagnosis, my mom read *Asperger's Syndrome* by Tony Attwood." He furthered shared the following:

> People ask me all the time why I've been successful and why others struggle, and why I've done well and all that. And I don't have the answer, to be quite fair, but I think I've always had ambitious goals. That are either for myself or, you know, were expected of me, whether it be my parents, or my school.
>   So, ambitious goals. I've always been told to shoot for the stars and hit the moon. The expectation was always high, and even though I was special, as in

special ed, and even though I had Asperger's and all this stuff. The standard was the same. My parents expected the same out of me. In fact, probably they expected in some ways, my mom would say no, they expected more out of me than even my brother. So, us, I think that's a lot of it. At the end of the day, that I think made the biggest difference.

Chapter Two

Learning Differences

According to the National Longitudinal Transition Study (2011), 60 percent of adults with disabilities reported continuing on to postsecondary education (any form of postsecondary education) within eight years of exiting high school. With the support that students with Autism Spectrum Disorders (ASD) receive through their Individualized Education Plans (IEPs), academic success at the secondary level is now common.

Camarena and Sarigiani (2009) mention the achievement of academic success in secondary school opens new doors for these students to advance into higher education; however, not all students with disabilities choose to disclose their disability in order to receive support in higher education. This makes it extremely difficult to estimate the exact percentage of students with ASD currently enrolled in higher education. Thus, higher-education institutions recently began to provide support services for the needs of these unique students.

This chapter will cover common learning differences college professors and staff might encounter while working with students with ASD. Students with ASD are all unique, so it is important to keep in mind that this is by no means an extensive list of learning differences. This chapter introduces additional common differences that are often puzzling to others.

Language Processing

The DSM-5 (APA, 2013) specified that receptive language often "lags" behind expressive language, so although an individual may understand communication, speech may be delayed. Schultz, Jacobs, and Schultz (2013) reported that individuals with ASD often demonstrate unusual or unique communication styles and have difficulty joining in conversation, which will often lead to a lifelong struggle with communication. Adreon and Durocher (2007) added that many individuals with ASD find change extremely difficult. This is particularly evident in conversation.

Schultz, Jacobs, and Schultz (2013) noted that the lack of predictability in conversation and social situations could cause individuals with ASD to withdraw. They added that tools such as social media are providing an outlet for communication skills development because individuals can interact electronically without the pressure of face-to-face interactions.

Emotional Language

According to Orsmond, Krauss, and Seltzer (2004), individuals with ASD have the most difficulty with nonverbal behaviors such as gestures and eye contact, and they do not understand how to respond to nonverbal cues appropriately. High-functioning individuals with ASD are able to interpret others' emotional behavior correctly and react with an appropriate emotional response if they are provided with explicit cues, in spite of their problems with spontaneous emotional interactions (Begeer et al., 2008).

Ironic Language

Verbal irony is when what is said is opposite than the literal meaning. Three types of verbal irony are sarcasm, overstatement, and understatement. Emphasis should be given to the social functions of ironic language when devising strategies to help children with ASD to deal with this complex aspect of everyday communication (Pexman et al., 2011).

Conrad spoke of the barriers to success that he, as a student with Asperger Syndrome, has faced in higher education. He commented:

> In my life, the biggest problem that I have is not being able to understand emotions. I don't know if you have ever seen *Big Bang Theory*, but I am kind of like Sheldon. I don't understand when people are being sarcastic; I don't understand when people are wanting to be comforted. You know, it is just really hard for me to understand emotions and sarcasm, so that is the biggest difficulty in making friends.
>
> Ever since *Big Bang Theory* came out, it has really helped me to give an example to what I am like to people. Before the show came out, everyone thought that I was weird or something because my jokes didn't make sense to them and their jokes didn't make sense to me. I didn't understand when they were making fun of me or when they were making a joke, so it was kind of hard and still is hard for me making friends.

Comprehension

Comprehension is frequently a concern for individuals with ASD. Many ASD individuals understand what they read but cannot effectively express what they know. There is no single strategy or method of teaching reading comprehension that will be 100 percent effective for individuals with ASD. Individuals diagnosed with ASD have unique learning needs and styles. The research shows that educators should use a variety of effective reading comprehension strategies based on the way each individual student with ASD learns best (Ball-Erickson, 2012).

Help in the Classroom

Success in college and beyond depends on one's ability to successfully communicate with others. It is imperative that college professors assist their students with ASD in developing better language skills in an attempt to be better prepared for the workplace once they earn their degree.

This can be accomplished with the use of technology and computer-based instruction in the classroom. Comprehension skills such as making inferences, distinguishing relevant information, and cause-and-effect relationships can all be supported by visual cues reinforced by the use of computer-assisted instruction for students with ASD (Ball-Erickson, 2012).

Facilitation of language skills can be done through the Disability Support Service center or the speech-language therapist on campus. If these services are not available, professors should work with their students to develop problem-solving skills, collaborative working skills, and professional etiquette skills.

Sensory Integration

Some individuals with ASD will react to stimuli differently than those who are not on the spectrum, and according to Case-Smith, Weaver, and Fristad (2015) approximately 80 percent of children with ASD are affected by sensory-processing problems. Sensory input, both hypo and hyper, is now a diagnostic criterion for ASD, according to the DSM-5 (2013).

Sensory integration dysfunction or disorder (SID) occurs when the brain has trouble receiving and responding to information that comes through the senses. Individuals who are affected by SID will overreact or underreact to stimuli. They may need more time to respond to stimuli because it takes them longer to process incoming stimuli.

Difficulties in sensory processing affect many aspects of the individual's life, including functioning in daily activities, learning, and behavior. Brushing teeth, sleeping, and eating are just a few daily activities that can be problematic for those with SID along with their ASD. Just as the symptoms of ASD vary with each individual, so do their SID symptoms.

According to Shankar, Smith, and Jalihal (2013), some individuals are more sensitive to their environments, and they are considered hypersensitive to outside stimuli. They may want to touch specific types of materials, or they want to avoid certain materials due to their texture, temperature, or consistency. Individuals may only want to eat certain foods because they avoid other types of foods that cause them discomfort. Hypersensitive individuals may find certain fabrics to be uncomfortable, so they only wear the same types of clothing.

While some individuals are more sensitive to their environment, others are less sensitive to their environments. Shankar, Smith, and Jalihal (2013) reported that those who suffer from hyposensitivity to outside stimuli require prompting because they do not know how to respond to a stimulus appropriately.

Individuals also may have difficulty with motor planning. For example, a person with SID may look extremely uncoordinated while running or participating in other physical activities. It is due to their SID, which could also cause them to be fatigued at a faster rate than that of their nondisabled peers.

Interventions

Interventions are usually sought for individuals with SID due to problematic behaviors. According to Devlin, Healy, Leader, and Hughes (2011), these behaviors often make it difficult to implement instructional programming, including placement in the least restrictive environment, and might cause injury to the individual or others in the environment.

Sensory integration therapy. Sensory Integration Therapy (SIT) is one type of therapy that is used as an intervention to help those who struggle with SID. According to Case-Smith, Weaver, and Fristad (2015), SIT is a clinic-based intervention that uses play activities and sensory-enhanced interactions to gain responses from a child. The purpose of the activities is to challenge the child's sensory processing and motor skills.

SIT is usually conducted in a clinic, using special equipment such as therapy balls, swings, trampolines, and others. It is through SIT that appropriate accommodations are made to an individual's environment, so that the student may self-regulate and participate in more of their daily activities.

Sensory-based intervention. Sensory-Based Intervention (SBI) is another type of therapy used to help those with SID. According to Case-Smith, Weaver, and Fristad (2015), SBI uses special equipment in the individual's natural environment instead of a clinic. For example, therapists may incorporate weighted and/or pressure vests, brushing, or methods in the individual's environment to promote self-regulation.

Help in the Classroom

The first way to help an individual with SID is to recognize that the underlying problem is due to his or her sensory processing. Often teachers will assume that the student simply has problem behavior. That is usually not the case. It is important to provide training to all staff members so that they can respond to problematic behaviors or other situations in an appropriate, informed manner.

For staff members who have students with SID in their classrooms, they must read documentation pertaining to each individual student. It is important to remember that to know one person with ASD and SID means you only know that person. Service providers will often provide blanket accommodations to all students who have the same eligibility or diagnosis. It is important to individualize accommodations based on each student's needs.

Students in higher education will be able to communicate their needs, but this is an area with which many students with ASD struggle. Professors can easily assist these struggling students by making small adjustments to what they already do in the classroom. According to Deris and Di Carlo (2013), classrooms should be organized, with a well developed schedule/routine.

Providing students with multiple modes of communication is especially helpful because some students will have difficulty talking to a professor; however, they may feel comfortable sending an e-mail. Professors need to be flexible. Students with ASD may encounter brand new stimuli in their classroom that they have never experienced before that causes them problems. Professors should be open to change and willing to accommodate the needs of each individual student.

Executive Functioning

Executive functions are a set of processes that allow individuals to set goals, organize themselves, and complete activities. These processes are often linked to an individual's ability to maintain emotional control and self-regulation. Executive dysfunctions occur when there is a disruption in the effectiveness of any of the executive functions. Students with ASD often experience executive dysfunctions that hinder their success and progress in college.

Executive dysfunctions may manifest themselves in several ways for students with ASD, including the inability to be flexible in certain situations, the difficulty in organizing one's self, and the misunderstanding of social communication. Rogers (2011) suggested that impairments in skill sets, which require response inhibition, working memory, and attention, are common executive dysfunctions found in both children and adults with ASD. This suggests that these are skill sets that most college students with ASD have struggled with for their entire lives.

Academic functioning is often greatly impacted by these students with lack of or poor management of executive functioning. There is no easy answer as to how to accommodate these issues; however, they are easily alleviated. Consideration from professors and staff on campus should be given when assisting a student with ASD to alleviate these issues. The simplest way to address this would be to bring the issue to the student's attention and teaching the student how to accommodate this on his or her own.

Time management. Many students with ASD struggle with time management when it comes to course management. They may struggle to see how to break the course requirements into sections so that they are not rushing at the end of the semester to finish the course requirements. If they are taking more than one course, they may have a hard time managing time to study and preparing for more than one exam that is given the same day or the same week.

Help in the Classroom

Professors and college staff can rectify these difficult times by assisting students with ASD on an individual basis to devise a plan for the best time management of their course. They can offer suggestions for study pacing and exam preparation. One may also offer to allow students with ASD to take their exam on an alternative day or time should they have multiple exams scheduled for the same day.

Organization. Organization is an additional executive function students with ASD often find baffling. They may have a difficult time organizing their location on campus and find themselves lost when trying to navigate from one location to another. Students with ASD also have a difficult time organizing their personal academic commitments. This can be a hindrance when they are trying to navigate an already difficult life, maintain friendships, and participate to the fullest extent possible in typical college life.

Help in the Classroom

Fortunately for students with ASD, colleges typically provide each student with a campus map, and many universities also offer public transportation on their campuses. If the college does not provide maps, one can easily be located in the campus police department.

Social participation is very important to many students with ASD; therefore, their attendance at events should be planned and encouraged. A discussion of how much time will be spent participating in social activities and frequent checks to determine if the students are actually participating in such events should be sufficient enough to show them the importance of being involved in campus life.

Social communication. According to Freedman (2010), students with ASD will oftentimes display their misunderstanding of social communication by talking about topics of interest to them even if the receiver is not interested in the topic. They may also struggle with "prosody," which is the pitch and inflection used in communicating with others. This may cause them to sound monotone or sometimes have a very high-pitched voice when speaking. Another major struggle for these students is that they interpret things they hear literally and have a difficult time interpreting humor and sarcasm.

Help in the Classroom

Many students with ASD will enter college with a misunderstanding of social communication even though they may have received years of language therapy from speech therapists prior to enrolling in the university. Professors and college staff can continue to address these issues by making a referral to someone on campus who is trained and licensed in working on pragmatic skills with adults. They can also remain patient and attempt to explain the situation when a student with ASD displays a misunderstanding of social communication.

These challenges can have a significant impact on the student's academic success. As a result of executive dysfunctions, many students will find themselves in a counterproductive routine from which they do not learn valid lessons. College students with ASD can overcome these counterproductive routines by establishing routines and living a life with structure. When shown coping strategies such as using a calendar, map, or bringing certain situations and issues to the students' attention, they are able to master these challenges, and they typically prove to be excellent college students.

CHAPTER HIGHLIGHTS

- There is no single strategy or method of teaching reading comprehension that is 100 percent effective for individuals with ASD.
- Difficulties in sensory processing can affect functioning in daily activities, learning, and behavior.
- Executive dysfunctions can easily be addressed by working individually with the students who may not even be aware they are experiencing these issues.

PONDER AND WONDER

1. Developing language skills in a population that naturally struggles with the skill set can be challenging. If your campus did not offer

support in language skill development, how would you assist students with ASD to develop the skills necessary to be successful in the workplace?

2. What type of training should university administrators provide for professors and staff that would assist ASD individuals who have sensory integration dysfunction (SID)?

3. If you had a student with ASD who was experiencing issues with one of the areas of executive functioning, how would you address the issue? Explain.

VOICES OF SUCCESS

Conrad shared the following regarding the barriers to success that he encountered as a student with Asperger Syndrome in higher education:

> My disability affects my learning in that it is hard for me to multitask. That is one of the big issues. It is very hard with the way it works for me. I need to be able to work on one thing. So, having to study for two or three exams on the same day was really hard. That affected my learning that way.
>
> It also affected me really bad. Like I said it is a communication disease, and I wouldn't understand some of the things that the teacher would say. I didn't know if they were being serious or not. I didn't know if they really wanted that assignment turned in that day, or if they were just joking. I didn't know if they really meant, "Oh, you should study that."
>
> Sometimes when teachers give subtle hints to things, I wouldn't be able to pick up on it. Everyone else knew what to study, and I wouldn't. I don't know why. If this has something to do with Asperger's or not, but I would miss hearing things all the time. I would go to take a test, and I would miss like five questions, because I never heard him say that we needed to know that and everyone else would be like, "Are you kidding, he said it right in class, and you were there." I don't know if that was because of Asperger's or that was something else, but it seems like that happened a lot.

Jimmy has always been academically gifted. He reported that many individuals on the spectrum feel very comfortable in academia, and he is one of those individuals. He loves learning, which is why he is pursuing his doctoral degree. Jimmy shared the following about his strengths and weaknesses in school:

> I've struggled to hand write. My hand hurts. I don't enjoy it. I jot short notes, but I never write anything. Writing a greeting card is about as much writing or writing a note card is about as much as I do. In college, all my notes were typed. I don't like cursive at all. They tried to teach me, and I got F's. I actually almost failed a grade because of cursive and spelling.

Of course, his mother did not let him fail, and she went to Jimmy's school and made sure that he was able to move on to the next grade. He was a straight A student, other than spelling and handwriting. Jimmy described one subject where he struggled:

> Math. I struggle with math, the abstract portion of it, which is unusual. I'm probably better at writing in English and imaginative, like creative writing type of stuff. History. I've always been fascinated with history. I love facts, love data. I've always really loved science, not chemistry, but like biology. Technology. I've always been fascinated by it. I love using new technology, buying the newest phone, newest computer.

Chapter Three

Self-Determination

Self-determination is a term that is commonly used in special education. Denney and Daviso (2012) and Carter, Owens, Trainor, Sun, and Sweeden (2009) reported that students with self-determination skills have better outcomes and a higher quality of life. For individuals to gain these skills, they need to have opportunities to develop them both at school and at home.

SELF-DETERMINATION DEFINED

Self-determination (SD) is defined as a combination of skills, knowledge, and beliefs that enable a person to engage in goal-directed, self-regulated, autonomous behavior. Self-determination also encompasses an understanding of ones' strengths and limitations combined with a belief that one is capable of being effective and successful. Self-determination is essential in enabling individuals to take control of their lives and participate in society (Field, Martin, Miller, Ward, & Wehmeyer, 1998).

Deci and Ryan (1985) developed Self-Determination Theory, which states that individuals need three things to be effective in their environment. They need to feel that they are effective (competence) in their environment, they must feel connected to others (relatedness), and they need to have freedom to follow their own interests and values (autonomy).

TEACHING SELF-DETERMINATION AT HOME

Burton-Hoyle (2011) explained that for parents of a typically developing child, planning for their needs is difficult; however, for the parents of a child with ASD, planning and developing self-determination skills can be overwhelming. Teaching these skills is not an easy process. It will often become very frustrating; however, it is necessary to teach them.

Choice. Choice is an opportunity for children to have power. Children should have opportunities to make their own choices. Something as simple as selecting an outfit, television program, or desserts are all choices that children can make at any age.

It is important for parents to accept the choices that children make. Parents who are concerned that their children will make outlandish decisions should provide them with two or three options so that the decisions or choices made are more structured. Although it is sometimes difficult for parents to give control to their children, these opportunities are necessary in order for students to develop confidence in their decision-making skills.

Social activities. Social activities can be difficult for individuals with ASD. Some feel that it is easier to avoid these situations rather than learn the skills needed to be more comfortable in these circumstances. ASD individuals often need direct instruction in social skills development. In order for these skills to be cultivated, opportunities need to be provided.

Parents can seek out opportunities in their community for social interaction with others. Church, sports, and martial arts are just a few suggestions. Many communities have support groups for families with children on the autism spectrum with scheduled activities for the children.

It is important for parents to pursue social activities for their ASD child even when these situations are not always easy. Children may act out, cause a scene, cry, or demonstrate other inappropriate and/or embarrassing behavior. Parents must continue providing these opportunities in order for their children to acquire the skills needed to be successful in social situations.

Independent living skills. Individuals with ASD need to be taught living skills so they can be as independent as possible. Domestic skills such as cleaning, cooking, and washing and drying laundry are all tasks that should be taught starting early on. Earning a driver's license is one of the greatest sources of independence a person can earn. Elliott described the freedom he enjoys from driving:

> I've only been driving for a week by myself. This is the first time I've ever had a car and just be driving wherever I need to go. Running errands and actually, I've bought more stuff alone this week that I probably have in my entire life. Yeah. Like, "Oh. I need to go and check about this price and this." I'm doing it, and it feels great!

It is important for parents and guardians to face the reality that they will not likely outlive their child(ren), so it is imperative to teach their child to be as independent as possible. Some individuals may never be able to live completely independently; however, parents can teach them the skills they need to be as independent as possible.

Support interests. Research has shown that ASD children learn more effectively when their parents engage them in activities that are based on their interests. The first step to determine a child's interests is to observe. This can be as simple as watching and monitoring the child's actions as well as interactions with others. Parents can use the following questions that will aide in identifying their child's interests.

- What excites your child?
- What makes your child happy?
- What is your child's favorite game?
- What does your child do at home on a regular basis?
- What activity keeps your child focused?

Once parents are aware of their child's interests, they can support them by providing daily activities. For example, if a child is interested in a musical instrument, simple daily activities can be planned to support this interest. The child can read books, learn how to play the instrument, visit a music store, and attend concerts. It is important to remember to encourage ASD children to vary their interests so that they are not fixated on one activity.

Goal setting. Setting goals is important for every college student. Individuals with ASD must set goals just like their peers; however, they should be encouraged to set academic goals, career goals, personal development goals, and social goals.

Setting these goals should be approached on an individual basis. Some students with ASD may need academic goals but not need support or goal setting in socialization. The important thing to remember about setting goals is that the goals should be set on an as-needed basis and reviewed and discussed frequently. Individuals with ASD must be reminded about their goals and how they are doing in reaching their goals.

If the goal is not appropriate, needs changes, or students are struggling with meeting the goal, it can be adjusted according to individual needs. Honest conversations about goal progress should occur frequently and serve as a gauge for goal progress.

TEACHING SELF-DETERMINATION AT SCHOOL

Schools are another great place for individuals to learn SD skills; however, self-determination will not be found as the lesson objective written on the classroom wall. Teaching self-determination skills occurs in the everyday routines and life experiences that students encounter. For students to receive opportunities to develop these skills, educators may need to think outside the box so that students are afforded these chances to grow and become more independent.

Choice. Giving students the opportunity of choice is a fantastic way for them to feel empowered in their education. For students on the spectrum, standing in front of the class and giving a report is not going to be an activity they would likely choose; however, if they were given another option for the project, they may feel more confident in their abilities and excitement for the project.

Students should also take an active role in their learning by being an active participant in their educational planning. They can do that by participating in their IEP meetings. It is there that students can choose their courses and discuss their accommodations. When students turn eighteen years old they assume their educational rights, unless their parents acquire guardianship or power of attorney. It is important to prepare students to take on this new role.

Strengths and weaknesses. Students with disabilities have both strengths and weaknesses; however, individuals will often find that they focus more on their weaknesses. For those on the spectrum, they need to know both their strengths and weaknesses at school and at home. Once a person can communicate their strengths and weaknesses and how their disability affects them, they can advocate for themselves more effectively. Greg discussed how knowing his disability was helpful:

> My thought is that the, the learning disability should not be considered a learning disability. I mean, so many people that have learning disability type things I went to school with, and they're leaps and bounds smarter than people I talk to in college. No offense, but I think it's part of it because some people understand themselves better.
>
> I think when you're little you have, you're kind of exposed to people coming to you and saying, "Hey. You got OCD, and that means you're gonna want to be always organized and type stuff like that." Then you get used to it, and you know what you need and what you like, stuff like that.

Temple Grandin (2007) recommended that students discover their areas of strength and focus on that area. She added that it is better to have more focus on strength then to strive for roundedness.

Likes and dislikes. Students with ASD often have strong opinions about their likes and dislikes. It is important to allow them ample time to explore both likes and dislikes. Just like their peers without ASD, they may be eager to participate in activities they like and less eager to participate in activities they dislike. It is important that families, friends, and faculty members show these students that just because they do not like something they must still participate in the activity.

Encouraging individuals with ASD to explore and participate in their dislikes can be a daunting task. If they are taught the importance of participating in activities they dislike early in their school careers, they will be more likely to participate. An example of this would be teaching them the importance of attending their peer's choir concert when they do not really like to listen to the choir simply because it is important to their peer.

Allowing students with ASD to explore their likes is a much easier task. They may only want to explore these tasks, and that can overcome any conversation they may have. It is important to assist them in finding a clear balance. Teaching them when it is appropriate to discuss their likes and how to manage their time spent doing things they like is the key to finding success.

Self-determination skills can be improved by allowing students with ASD to make choices pertaining to their likes and dislikes. They should be allowed to have input and make choices about what they want to study after secondary school. Their thoughts and goals should be front and center when developing transition plans. When students with ASD are allowed to make choices for their future, they are more likely to have success in programs in which they are enrolled.

Social activities. Social activities can take place in the school setting. Students can attend or participate in extracurricular activities. School programs and dances are also opportunities for ASD students to socialize with their peers. Prior to the events, the teacher can talk about the event, the people, and the social activity.

The teacher can also model the appropriate behaviors related to specific settings and have the student mimic or model the desired behavior. The teacher can rehearse a plan for the student to follow or use if the setting becomes overwhelming or is not enjoyable. Signals or cues can be used to indicate that the child is uncomfortable and ready to leave.

OPPORTUNITIES. OPPORTUNITIES. OPPORTUNITIES.

Everyone has heard the saying "practice makes perfect." The more opportunities individuals with ASD are given to practice and develop their SD skills, the stronger their skills become. It is never too early for individuals to start building these skills. It is also never too late to start learning; however, some habits may need to be broken.

CHAPTER HIGHLIGHTS

- Self-Determination Theory states that individuals need the following three things to be effective in their environment: Individuals need to feel that they are effective (competence), they must feel connected to others (relatedness), and they need to have freedom to follow their own interests and values (autonomy).

- Individuals with ASD should have opportunities to make their own choices.
- Students with ASD learn more effectively when their parents engage them in activities that are based on their interests.

PONDER AND WONDER

1. How can an instructor tailor an assignment or project based on the interest of an ASD student?
2. When assigning oral class presentations, what alternative assignment can instructors provide for ASD students? Should all students have the opportunity to select the alternate assignment?

VOICES OF SUCCESS

Jimmy described his strengths and weaknesses at home, particularly organization and cleanliness, in the following way:

> Orderly, ordered, structured like. For instance, my desk, everything was straight. Everything had a style. I arranged things. Like even on my desk now, like I have a certain arrangement of things, and if my wife switched it on me, it'd bother me, and I'd notice. I'm technically a little compulsive about organizing things and filing things and sorting things.
>
> I still am to this day. Definitely not as bad as I used to be. I used to have a hard time with one particular social skill when I was a kid, and that was that I had friends come over, and I want to, I literally wanted to write out a schedule and structure our playtime together. And somewhat like an itinerary, I'm not kidding. I'd type it on the computer and print it out, and they'd come over, and I'd say, "Here is what we're doing this weekend," and I'd hand this over.

Since Abigail was not diagnosed with autism until after high school, she was not able to access supports while in school. However, after her diagnosis, she has received support through vocational rehabilitation centers. In a conversation with Abigail, she was asked what helped her make the decision to go to college. Thoughtfully, she responded:

> There was no family support. I was the first person in my family to go to college. I was very active in youth leadership in the Methodist church. And, then it came time for me to go to college. The youth pastor had left our local church and become the pastor for the campus of this little Methodist college I went to.

Once he got involved there, he decided he was going to kind of rescue me, so he recruited me to come to school there. It was the best thing he could have done. He got me out of the house, and we had no money, so I was eligible for a full package.

I mean, it was sort of like I woke up one day, and I was at college. You know, I don't remember anyone during college or anyone in high school actually discussing a concept like a career or employment or what do you want to do. It was just, oh it's college, and this is what I do next. There was no global thinking. I think my mother was frankly shocked when I came home and told her I was applying, because that just wasn't even on their radar.

Chapter Four

Passing the Baton through Transition Planning

Planning for the future of a child is difficult, and it is often overwhelming for parents of children with a disability. In an effort to support individuals with disabilities and improve their postsecondary outcomes, the Individuals with Disabilities Educational Act (2004) included a mandate for schools to provide transition planning for all students who receive special education services.

What is transition planning, and how does it help students and their parents? It is defined in the law as:

> A results-oriented process, that is focused on improving the academic and functional achievement of the child with a disability to facilitate the child's movement from school to post-school activities, including postsecondary education, vocational education, integrated employment (including supported employment); continuing and adult education, adult services, independent living, or community participation. (IDEA, 2004)

The law requires transition planning to start at the age of sixteen; however, the starting age varies by state. Some states recognized that early planning would result in better outcomes, so the Texas Legislature passed Senate Bill 1788 (2011), which lowered the required transition age to fourteen.

Roberts (2010) listed topic areas to be addressed during transition planning as "career exploration, academic goal setting and preparation, assessing and identifying learning styles, self-advocacy skills, reasonable accommodations, academic supports, interagency collaboration, technology, and time management" (p. 159). The purpose is to provide a student with a "seamless transition" into the adult world, which may be higher education or employment.

Hendricks and Wehman (2009) discovered that personnel who are usually responsible for completing the secondary transition services are classroom teachers, and they added that those who are charged with transition planning need to carefully address the needs of those with ASD. Ideally, a team of professionals, the student, and the parents of the student actively participate in transition planning.

GOALS

Hendricks and Wehman (2009) explained that the driving force behind a transition plan relies on the development of goals. The goals may change throughout the student's transition time, so it is important for the person who is writing the plan to conduct assessments to aid students in discovering strengths, weaknesses, and interests.

Postsecondary goals. The first type of goal is the postsecondary goal, which includes a career goal, training/education needed to reach that goal, and an independent living goal when appropriate. Postsecondary goals need to include independent living goals for when the individual outlives his or her parents (Barnhill, 2007).

Postsecondary goals should be realistic, which may be disheartening to a student. However, a transition specialist can help students find careers in their areas of interest. That is why appropriate assessments are so important. There are numerous assessments that can be conducted to determine a student's strengths and weaknesses while paying attention to their likes and dislikes. Also, agencies such as the Department of Assistive and Rehabilitative Services (DARS) will conduct assessments so they can provide job development that is appropriate for the student.

Annual goals. Hendricks and Wehman (2009) added that the transition specialist, usually a classroom teacher, will also work with the student to develop annual goals. The annual goals include a coordinated set of activities to work toward the student's postsecondary goals. For example, if a student is interested in the medical field, then he or she should take a health class or nursing class in high school.

It is recommended that annual goals included in the transition plans for students with ASD focus on the development of communication skills, social skills, and community involvement. Shogren, Wehmeyer, and Palmer (2013) recommended that students need to be provided repeated opportunities to practice setting goals in all aspects of their lives, not only for transition planning purposes.

Summary of performance. IDEA (2004) included a mandate for schools to include a Summary of Performance (SOP) to the transition plan of students who were graduating or aging out of secondary school. According to IDEA (2004), the SOP is defined as "a summary of the child's academic achievement and functional performance, which shall include recommendations on how to assist the child in meeting their postsecondary goals."

Steere and DiPipi-Hoy (2013) clarified that IDEA 2004 did not provide any guidelines on how the SOP should look. They advised that it should be completed during the student's final IEP meeting, before exiting special education in secondary school. This will ensure that the student's most updated "skills, abilities, and needs" are outlined for the agencies that will provide services for the student after exiting secondary education.

COLLABORATION

Early collaboration between schools and adult agencies is the key to successful transition. Transition is often very difficult for youth with ASD and their families. Students and families should become educated about the community agencies that are available to young adults with ASD.

One obstacle for families is that there is not one agency that is completely devoted to autism and to access services. Students and their families must contact multiple agencies to investigate their eligibility and services (Hagner et al., 2012; McDonough & Revell, 2010). It is difficult, frustrating, and overwhelming for families to navigate the numerous agencies to determine services after high school.

When families and students are provided the linkage to the agencies while the student is still in school, then the transition to adult services is much smoother. It is important for the schools to help families identify the adult agencies that will provide the postsecondary students the services they need.

EARLY LINKAGE TO AGENCIES

Agencies provide numerous services for those with disabilities such as job training, supportive living, respite care, and others. Schools need to stress the importance of early registration to families. There are currently ten-to-twelve-year waiting lists for some services, so it is crucial that children are registered when they are young. This means elementary age or younger. For students who do not register until high school, they may be waiting until their late twenties or early thirties before they start receiving services.

For some parents, it is difficult to think that far into the future. They may still be in shock or denial about their child's diagnosis. Other parents may think that they will be able to take care of their child forever, and they do not consider the fact that their child will probably outlive them. Often parents will assume other family members or siblings will care for their child. However, that is not a fair assumption.

To effectively link parents with agencies, schools should do more than just handing parents a list with contact information. Instead, school personnel should offer to make the call for them or invite agency representatives to IEP meetings. Schools should remind parents that when services are offered for their child, they have the option to refuse assistance. It is better to have the preference because they do not know what their lives will look like in ten to twelve years.

END OF ENTITLEMENT

When a student leaves secondary education, they are no longer entitled to the services that were provided during school. This is the reason that students with disabilities need to participate in their transition planning so that they may advocate for themselves. In order to gain services in higher education, the student must seek out the services.

Students with disabilities must advocate and access the services and supports they have a right to on their own; they must also make themselves known to the person or persons responsible for providing the necessary accommodations (Ciccantelli, 2011; Wolf et al., 2009). Many students with disabilities, including those with ASD or AS, do not consider themselves disabled. They simply see themselves as different and therefore do not disclose their disability or advocate for the necessary accommodations, according to Schlabach (2008). Schlabach indicated that students with disabilities who access support services at their higher-education institution are more likely to graduate from college.

CHAPTER HIGHLIGHTS

- Transition planning is legally mandated for any student with a disability starting at the age of sixteen.
- Early collaboration between schools and adult agencies is the key to successful transition.
- When a student leaves secondary education, they are no longer entitled to services provided under their IEP. Students with disabilities must register with the office for support services on their campus to determine what accommodations and/or modifications they require on their college campus.

PONDER AND WONDER

1. As an educator, how can you assist in making transition planning easier for the families of individuals with ASD?
2. At times, school districts invite agencies to participate in transition planning, but the agencies do not participate. In your opinion, what could be done to improve agency participation and linkages?

VOICES OF SUCCESS

During Bernard's enrollment in public schools, he was able to receive special education services due to his disability. He was asked if he attended his annual ARD meetings, and if he did, did he participate and help make decisions concerning his educational planning. Bernard remembered going to his ARD meetings, and he was able to pick classes that interested him. He did not recall taking part in his transition planning.

Bernard has been linked with agencies while he has been at school and also since he has graduated. While still in school, he attended summer programs through the local MHMR center, and he currently participates in social gatherings and field trips through the center. Bernard mentioned several field trips he attended, including dates. He has also linked with DARS, and his counselor has helped him gain services in college, along with the office of disabilities at the campus he attends.

During Elliott's enrollment in public schools, he was able to receive special education service due to his disability. He was also asked if he attended his annual ARD meetings, and if he did, did he participate and help make decisions concerning his educational planning. He responded:

> I did the ARD since sixth grade onward. As the years went on, I started talking more. Because sixth and seventh grade I didn't talk. I just listened. I kind of, I kind of agreed with whatever the teachers said was good for me. I never really kind of put my own voice into what I was gonna do, and then I finally started getting my own voice to say, "I want this."

When discussing Elliott's participation in his transition planning for life after high school, he recalled:

> I did. We had two ARD meetings. I know we did that. We did, they did let me talk about the transition and about what I wanted in college and after high school. So I did have a voice in my transition planning.

Elliott was often frustrated in planning meetings because committee members were pushing him to go to community college or technical school first, but he was set on going to the local university. Elliott also added that he was linked with DARS, and he had already met with the disabilities office at his university for accommodations.

Chapter Five

Communication Challenges

Communication is an area of difficulty for many individuals on the spectrum. Higher education requires communication to occur in multiple facets, and for the majority of these students, this is the first time that these individuals are completely in charge of their educational programming. Parents who have acted as their child's advocate and voice are no longer able to speak for their child since they have now reached the age of majority. This is a new role for these students.

According to Schultz, Jacobs, and Schultz (2013), lack of understanding of personal space, difficulty in understanding the perspective or intentions of others, and inabilities to distinguish sincere interactions from those meant to hurt, use, or mock can cause lifelong communication and interaction struggles.

Understanding the struggles of these students is essential for faculty and staff in higher education. While there are no set rules to follow when students struggle to communicate, there are aspects of the communication struggle that can be eased with assistance. In chapter 1, we briefly discussed communication skills for college students with ASD.

This chapter will further investigate communication skills and provide insight into the struggles that commonly occur in higher education. Simple steps that can be taken to make these struggles a less pronounced part of these individuals' lives are addressed in this chapter.

COMMUNICATION WITH PROFESSORS

Numerous students with ASD have difficulties with verbal and nonverbal communication (American Psychiatric Association [APA], 2013). Some concerns include having problems taking turns during conversations, tone of voice, and difficulty comprehending figurative language, and some students seldom or never speak. Students with ASD are comfortable being alone and often have difficulty reading social cues (APA, 2013).

It is the responsibility of ASD students to seek support services in higher education. The reasons for providing assistance and accommodations in the classroom is to ensure that students with disabilities are successful and have an equal opportunity to access the material as their nondisabled peers (Freedman, 2010). The faculty and staff at the higher-education institution are key players in implementing support services for students with disabilities (Wolf et al., 2009).

Students requiring assistance should contact their individual campus' Office of Services for Students with Disabilities. Services are designed to assure students with disabilities have equal access to the university's activities, programs, and services. Some of the services provided include academic accommodations, assistive equipment, communication access service providers, note takers, physical access, and priority registration.

Documentation of a disability from a professional in the field is required to receive services. Students with disabilities should notify the director of the Office of Services for Students with Disabilities prior to registration in any university program. The director will arrange a meeting with the student to determine an individualized educational plan.

Although individuals with ASD are varied and require individualized support, they tend to think literally and require very specific directives. Many ASD students require more specific directions. Stating that an assignment is due next week is not always enough information for ASD students. Instead, the professor can state that everyone should submit his or her assignment to Blackboard by a specific due date. Giving the directions to the entire class will not single out any ASD students.

Professors can consider the following accommodations for ASD students:

- Allow extra time for students to submit assignments.
- Provide students with options for oral presentations.
- Allow students the option to work individually when assigning group projects.
- Allow students the option of using computers to complete assignments versus pencil and paper.
- Allow students time to schedule appointments to meet during hours or be available before and after class for individualized questions.

Professors should also plan class lectures and discussions with ASD students in mind. Directions for all assignments should always be clear and concise. Written class notes or outlines should be readily available. Professors are highly encouraged to meet with the director of the Office of Services for Students with Disabilities for assistance with accommodations and course planning.

COMMUNICATION WITH CAMPUS PERSONNEL

In addition to professors, ASD students may have difficulty communicating with campus personnel including police officers, dorm or apartment managers, dining hall staff, librarians, and others. Many ASD students have trouble understanding facial and body expressions. Maintaining eye contact during conversations is also an issue for some ASD students. The students may be reluctant to ask for help and also in expressing their thoughts.

All university personnel who interact with ASD individuals should receive training on suggested communication techniques. Some ASD students will wait for verbal or physical prompts. The students eventually become dependent on the cues. Creating an awareness of the communication concerns faced by ASD individuals will bring light to issues that have often been overlooked.

COMMUNICATION WITH PEERS

Students with ASD have difficulty with both verbal and nonverbal communication, which affects social skills. Schultz, Jacobs, and Schultz (2013) noted that the lack of predictability in conversation and social situations could cause individuals with ASD to withdraw.

These individuals also have limited interests, and they tend to dominate conversations with their own interests. They neglect to include the interests and thoughts of others in the conversation, and reciprocal conversations are awkward. Continued practice in conversation is the best way to develop these skills.

Many institutions of higher education offer support groups to students with ASD. They meet weekly, and they discuss things going in their lives and at school. Students have the opportunity to discuss issues they may be having, and they can use this time to brainstorm strategies to deal with situations.

Cooperative learning. During college, students will have courses that require them to participate in group projects. Not only do students have to work together as a team and produce a product, they must be able to communicate with the members of the group. Zeedyk, Tipton, and Blacher (2014) affirmed that this high level of social engagement is particularly difficult for those on the spectrum.

In discussing cooperative learning with Murphy, he shared the following thoughts regarding group projects:

Intellectually, I have always been very strong. Socially, learning is very difficult. I have trouble with group projects. I don't do really well with group projects. First of all, when I was younger I was always the kid that got all the work hoisted on them while everyone else did nothing. As an adult, grad school projects seem better to me because everyone else pulls their weight.

Even as an undergraduate, I mean even at the college level, I am like a senior in college and these people are still like can you do the work? Finally, when I was a senior I got to where I would say no it is your part of the project. It took me a very long time to have enough self-confidence to say don't ask me what to write; I told you that we divided this up.

This is your part, here is the basic idea what we are saying in this paper, now you write it. I can't tell you what is right. I am, like, you are a freshman, you don't understand what I am doing right now. How much research I am doing right now? I don't have time for you and your little petty paper. I just never really, I prefer working alone when I could because I just liked to really do the research. I love to write so those go well together.

When it comes to working with people it is always tough. Growing up, I felt like people were like making fun of me and all that. They were not very nice to me, so I am always nervous now as an adult in group projects. I am always like do I talk now? Do I talk too much? I think group projects are probably the biggest anxiety problem for me. I get very scared.

Anything where I have to talk to people I get very nervous. Like work in a group, function in a group, because I just worry about am I doing it right? Are these people judging me? Do they actually hate me? Are they making fun of me? That whole kind of thing.

Relationships. Individuals with ASD often find social interactions difficult, and they generally have difficulty developing and maintaining friendships. Shattuck et al. (2007) found that the most common symptom of ASD was the lack of friendships or mutual relationships among those with ASD.

Some college students have positive experiences with peers in higher education because they are able to meet with individuals with whom they share common interests. Tools such as social media are providing an outlet for communication skills development because individuals can interact electronically without the pressure of face-to-face interactions.

Roommates. Students with ASD may choose to live on campus during their time in college. Typically, roommates are chosen after students complete an interview form, and students are matched based on interests. Students with disabilities can request accommodations for their housing.

Ackles, Fields, and Skinner (2013) reported that residential living can be complicated for this population of students because they have to make the following adjustments to campus living: organization, building peer relationships, independent living, and shared living quarters.

Some college campuses offer six-week transition periods for new students, instead of the typical three-day orientation. This type of program would be beneficial for those with ASD so they can get accustomed to campus life, which includes campus living. They can also use this time to get to know the campus.

WRITTEN COMMUNICATION

Many individuals with ASD struggle with written communication throughout their life. Writing stories, essays, reports, journal entries, copying notes, and papers can be stressful tasks for those on the spectrum. Although these students have a strong vocabulary, the writing process is a struggle. They also strain to physically write.

The writing process. Prewrite, draft, revise, edit, and publish. These are the steps students learn for the writing process, and for those with ASD, the difficulties start with the very first step. According to Asaro-Saddler and Bak (2014), individuals on the spectrum have limited interests. Because of this, students may have a hard time choosing a subject to write on that will meet the requirements of the writing assignment.

If given the opportunity to write on a topic of their own choosing, students will often have an easier time getting started. Students tend to write more descriptively when they are able to write on topics that pique their interests.

Physical writing. Many individuals with ASD have motor and coordination issues that make writing difficult. According to Asaro-Saddler and Bak (2014), while some individuals have good ideas, handwriting is so difficult, and sometimes painful, that their writing is affected. Jimmy explained his experiences with writing:

> I've struggled to hand write, my hand hurts. I don't enjoy it. I jot short notes but I never write anything. Like writing about a greeting card is about as much writing or writing a note card is about it as much as I do. So yes, writing has always been a barrier for me; it still is because it's handwritten.

Students like Jimmy will often receive occupational therapy to help them with their handwriting skills. Students could also work with assistive technology such as laptops, tablets, and word processors to complete written assignments. Students may also receive extended time to complete written assignments as an accommodation.

Writing supports. There are several options for students to get help with their writing in higher education. The greatest obstacle for these students is that they have to seek the services out, which may be difficult for them. The first source from which a student can receive assistance is their professor. Students can e-mail, call, or make an appointment with their professor so they can gain some clarity on assignments.

Most institutions of higher education have writing centers where students can access assistance with their writing. Tutorials are often provided free to students, and they can be presented either in face-to-face meetings or via online conferencing. Writing centers also provide writing workshops to help students improve their writing skills.

For students who continue struggling, they can meet with their Office of Disabilities counselor to strategize and gain more support. It may be necessary for them to take a developmental writing course if they continue to struggle with their writing skills. Also, accommodations may need to be adjusted for the student.

CHAPTER HIGHLIGHTS

* Communication is an essential life skill that the vast majority of individuals with ASD struggle with across settings.
* Although individuals with ASD are varied and require individualized support, they tend to think literally and require very specific directives.
* Many ASD students have trouble understanding facial and body expressions.

PONDER AND WONDER

1. A professor noticed that a student experienced difficulty communicating in class. Based on prior training, the professor noticed signs of ASD. The professor had not received notification from the Office of Services for Students with Disabilities indicating that the student has been identified with a disability. What steps should the professor take to assist the struggling student?
2. Many required university trainings are conducted online. In planning an online training for university personnel in assisting ASD individuals, what targeted areas would you recommend in the area of communication?

VOICES OF SUCCESS

As Olivier finished describing ways he has found success, he spoke of the barriers to his success. He commented:

> When I give a speech sometimes I can kind of stutter along, but when I am working with what I like to do it doesn't. I can also see that there are people who talk equality and this is a very liberal school. There are people that talk all about equality, and people are trying to force equality on everybody even

though that is not exactly what I believe. That is probably things, the political stuff, it's all good.

I have never asked for support and not received it. One of the things that others might face is, like communication disabilities, that is probably the most common. They don't make eye contact when they speak with you.

Conrad commented on what strategies students with HFA or AS can implement to overcome barriers in higher education. He suggested the following, "Let them know right away. Don't wait for there to be a problem. Let them know before you even start the class that you have this problem."

Chapter Six

Time Management

Management skills are a necessity for college students. Students are given deadlines for class assignments, and professors and instructors expect everyone to submit the assignments in a timely manner. Hughes (2009) suggested that before students with ASD actually begin classes, they are encouraged to participate in orientation and tour the campus to learn where important points of interest are, specifically the Disability Office, so they can know where to go for help.

COURSE MANAGEMENT

Academic advisors are instrumental in ensuring that ASD students are provided with support to ensure their success. The advisors' role is to provide students with information regarding course requirements and needed resources. Academic advisors should strongly encourage ASD students to seek services that will provide the accommodations needed for the students' scheduled courses. Due to the increasing number of college students with ASD, there is an apparent need for advisors to be aware of the kind of support students with ASD may require (Smith, 2007; Taylor, 2005).

Strategies for academic advisors. The following strategies are suggested for advisors in assisting students with ASD:

- Review ASD students' records to obtain as much information as possible regarding their disability.
- Initially recommend classes that offer assistance to first-year students. Many universities provide courses for new students that focus on transitioning to college life. Note-taking and time-management strategies are addressed during the success courses.

- Recommend that ASD students are paired with a student mentor and if possible a faculty mentor.
- Provide assistance regarding test-taking procedures.
- Meet with students throughout the semester and monitor their progress.
- Encourage ASD students to seek services from the Office of Services for Students with Disabilities.

Managing multiple classes. Students with ASD have difficulty with time management, particularly in the area of course management. The students may struggle in managing how to divide the course requirements into sections so that they can complete all assigned tasks by the end of the course. If they are taking multiple courses, they may face difficulty managing time to study and prepare for assignments in all classes.

Professors should be cognizant of a student's ASD disability so they can assist the student by providing organization and structure to lectures. According to Hart and Brehm (2013), it is important to determine what postsecondary success is based on the individual. For example, students may need to audit classes and learn independent living skills such as travel training, financial literacy, and social skills development. These skills would be considered a successful college experience because individuals will be increasing their independence.

Turning in assignments on time. ASD students are encouraged not wait until the last minute to work on assignments or study for an exam. Students are advised to complete assignments early to avoid the stress in rushing at the last minute. In discussing time management with Conrad, he stated, "Time management is kind of crucial when you have this disability because if you don't manage it, you get overwhelmed really easily, and if you get overwhelmed you just can't function."

SCHEDULING TIME TO WORK AND STUDY

ASD students can keep track of their schedules using monthly calendars. Calendars can be in print or electronic format. The selection should be the preference of the student. It is suggested that students use calendars that show one month at a time. This will allow ASD students to visualize their plans for the day, week, and month. Students should record the due dates and times for assignments, projects, papers, and exams. They can also notate daily study hours on the calendar.

ORGANIZATIONAL SKILLS

Binders are a class necessity for organizing class notes and handouts. ASD students can simplify their class information by using a separate binder for each class. Students can also use electronic portfolios as an option for organizing class materials. Class schedules and syllabi should also be included in the binders or electronic portfolios.

In discussing the importance of organizing class materials, Paris shared the following in regard to her organizational skills:

> Students should kind of figure out what they are interested in, and what works for them. As far as studying and academics go, just pursue it. For me, at least one of the big deals was time management. In high school your days are broken up into like fifty-minute blocks, and you know exactly what you are going to do, but in college that was not the case at all. I found that I had to use my phone and make a to-do list and just, like, plan out every day to the half.
>
> I planned when I would be in class and when I had rehearsal. Other people thought I was crazy, but that was the only way I would get things done and accomplish them the way I needed to. I think that is a big thing to figure out what works for you; if it is setting reminders in your computer, or keeping a notebook, or having a friend text you and say hey, remember to hand that in, that was helpful.

PREPARING FOR EXAMS

Students who have notified the Disability Services Office are encouraged to meet with their professors at the beginning of the semester to discuss all accommodations, particularly for exams. The most common accommodations reported as being provided by higher-education institutions were (1) extended time on tests, (2) tests taken in a quiet setting, (3) tutoring, (4) study center assistance, and (5) technology aids such as assistive technology and the use of a computer lab (Freedman, 2010).

If possible, students could view examples of previous exams to note the format and expectations of the test. If the exam is given in a different setting, the ASD student must be informed of the room design. Anything that might cause anxiety must be addressed prior to the exam. In addition to exams, faculty are encouraged to move beyond grades and focus on developing students' skills in self-instruction, self-regulation, and problem solving (Hong, Haefner, & Slekar, 2011).

TIME MANAGEMENT TIPS

The following are suggested time management tips for ASD college students:

- Locate a quiet setting to study and complete assignments. The environment should be conducive for the individual student.
- Use calendars in planning times for daily schedules. Electronic devices such as cell phones and computers can also be used to provide daily reminders.
- Develop a daily routine.
- Divide assignments and projects into sections.
- Check schedules each morning and review throughout the day.
- Update and revise schedules when unexpected events occur.

CHAPTER HIGHLIGHTS

- Academic advisors are instrumental in ensuring that ASD students are provided with support to ensure their success.
- Students with ASD have difficulty with time management, particularly in the area of course management.
- ASD students are encouraged to use calendars, binders, electronic portfolios, cell phones, and computers to assist with time management and organization.

PONDER AND WONDER

1. How can professors assist online ASD students with test preparation?
2. How should professors address an ASD student who frequently submits assignments late without requesting an extension?
3. How can universities ensure that academic advisors are meeting the needs of ASD students?

VOICES OF SUCCESS

Russell voiced his thoughts on time management. He indicated the following in his message:

> To make the college experience better I would probably get a small schedule that would be comfortable. Basically, that would accommodate them to where it won't send them into distress. It won't be really anything strenuous. Get it depending on what class they are taking. Extending times and getting certain accommodations may be in order.
>
> I believe any autistic children, almost always an autistic child can attend college, even children with Asperger's Syndrome and high functioning. They can do it, it is just trying to adjust to change. Because change is very difficult for us, a lot of autistic children have a certain routine like regular children.

They go to school, they come home, watch TV, do homework. It almost seems everlasting for them and trying to break that barrier, it's really hard.

Conrad voiced his thoughts on time management:

The biggest obstacle is multitasking, being able to study for more than one thing at a time and not overwhelming yourself. It was always easier on me in college when I took like three or four classes a semester as opposed to five or six.

Chapter Seven

Developing Relationships

Developing relationships is a key component to success in college for all students. Individuals with ASD often struggle with developing relationships due to the fact that their communication skills are not as well developed as others. Social interactions can be confusing and difficult for students with ASD, which makes it difficult to develop relationships.

Realistically, there are no answers as to how to best help students with ASD develop relationships while in college, but there are several things college faculty and staff can do to assist students with this process. Campus relationships are just as important as personal relationships for students with ASD; therefore, careful planning and support can generate positive relationship experiences.

CAMPUS RELATIONSHIPS

Hughes (2009) suggested that before students with ASD actually begin classes, they need to participate in orientation and tour the campus to learn where important points of interest are, specifically the Disability Office, so they can know where to go for help. Thus, students should participate in early arrival programs (Ackles, Fields, & Skinner, 2013). Professors need to be aware of a student's ASD disability so they can also assist the student as needed, which could include suggesting a student visit the writing center for tutoring, assigning peer tutors to the student, and providing organization and structure to lectures so the student with ASD can follow it more easily (Hughes, 2009).

Faculty. The front line of defense for individuals with ASD is faculty. These individuals are asked to provide accommodations and offer strategies and support for their students with ASD on an individual basis. A positive and trusting relationship between faculty and students with ASD is very important.

Relationships between faculty and students with ASD are best formed on an individual basis. The direct interaction may require some support from the Office of Disability Services. Some faculty may be experiencing working with a student with ASD for the first time. Behaviors may not be typical and interactions may be strained; therefore, faculty should be trained on supporting positive relationships with both students who have ASD and the Office of Disability Services.

When a campus experiences an enrollment increase of students with ASD, it is imperative that all members of the faculty and academic administrators work together to devise a plan to support these students. Understanding the needs of these students will allow for a seamless transition from one faculty member to another. Faculty also must feel supported by their administration in assisting these students in their classrooms.

Wolf, Brown, and Bork et al. (2009) suggested administration support faculty by using "teachable moments" with faculty when an incident with a student arises. They also suggested developing letters and fact sheets to share important information pertaining to educating these students. Outside agencies can also provide training and support to assist faculty in meeting the needs of these students.

It is important to remember that faculty is often uncomfortable handling the unique situations students with ASD bring to their classrooms. They are expected to accommodate and be sympathetic to behaviors and demands that would be unacceptable in other situations. Having an underlying understanding of students with ASD will allow faculty to meet the demands and needs of this unique population.

Developing an underlying understanding will require some planning and training on the part of the college administration. There are always outside agencies that are willing to help train college faculty, but sometimes the best trainers come from within a faculty. Members of the special education faculty and staff in the office of Disability Support Service can be beneficial in providing basic training, usually free of charge, to students with ASD and their needs in college.

Campus personnel. In addition to working with faculty, students with ASD must interact with other campus personnel such as members of the residence staff, cafeteria staff, and security. These personnel will require the same type of underlying understanding of individuals with ASD as professors and administration. Developing relationships with these personnel will ensure that students with ASD are comfortable with their surroundings.

After training campus personnel on the basics of students with ASD, a plan to develop relationships with these students should be put into place. This plan can include certain people within each department who are willing to become the contact for students with ASD. This person should have a clear understanding of these students and a willingness to put the time into developing relationships.

Not all students with ASD will disclose their disability to university personnel. This will make it difficult to identify a point of contact for students with ASD. Campus personnel can be trained in responding to behavior typical to students with ASD and making a referral to the contact person. This person can then make it a point to meet with the individual in question. Developing a relationship with this student, regardless of ASD, is beneficial.

PERSONAL RELATIONSHIPS

According to Henault (2005), adolescents and adults with ASD are interested in having friendships and sexual relationships. They are also interested in marriage and should be given the opportunities to develop relationships that will eventually lead to these relationships (Newport & Newport, 2002).

Family relationships are developed long before a student reaches college. There are stark differences for student with ASD as far as family relationships go. These students and families are accustomed to the family (typically mother) handling and requesting all of the students' needs. Adjusting to college life can be difficult for both the student and parents.

Peers. Students with ASD desire to have relationships with their peers just as much as the typically developing college student. These relationships require support and understanding on the part of others. Many individuals with ASD will allow themselves to be isolated out of sheer discomfort.

Faculty can support students with ASD in developing relationships with their peers by informing them of upcoming activities for clubs and organizations within their college. They can also encourage participation in volunteer opportunities given to students throughout the semester. Faculty support in developing peer relationships will also increase trust from the student with ASD.

Many dorms offer activities that give students the opportunity to connect with others. These activities are often confusing and too fast paced for students with ASD. Staff at the dorm can easily let the student with ASD know about the event and what the event will entail ahead of time. This will provide an opportunity for the student to plan for the activity and think about the appropriate social responses to such an activity.

Families. It is not necessary for students with ASD to develop new relationships with family members once they reach college; however, it is necessary for students to develop different relationships with their family. The dynamic of college life leaves students with ASD with a different set of

needs from their families than they have ever had before. This can be difficult for both the student and the family.

Faculty and staff can assist students with ASD in developing different
relationships with their families by offering information sessions for both
students and their families before the semester begins. Topics in these trainings should be very similar to a typical orientation but include information on
the rights and responsibilities of college students. Discussion may take place
about different programs that are offered for students with ASD on that
particular campus.

Families should foster independence in their student long before that
student steps foot on a college campus. Even with this independence, faculty
and staff must stress the importance of continuous monitoring of academic
and social progress while their student is away at college.

According to Conrad, his family was very good at checking with him on a
regular basis. He explains that his mother would call him weekly and ask
several very simple questions that kept him focused on both his academics
and socialization. He shared the following:

> One of the things we, as a family, did is ask questions. Are you making
> friends? Are you doing your work consistently? Are you doing this, that, and
> other? Are you hanging out with people? Stuff like that. Autism is mainly a
> communication thing.

Dating. Faculty and staff are not responsible for assisting students with
ASD in developing personal relationships with someone they would be interested in dating. Students with ASD may find themselves interested in dating
and possibly marriage for the first time once they reach college. They may
turn to a trusted member of their school's faculty and staff for dating and/or
marriage advice.

Faculty and staff should be prepared with background knowledge of dating struggles for individuals with ASD. They should have knowledge of
programs or people on campus students can talk to about their interests in
dating. If a student comes to them for advice and they feel ill prepared to
handle the situation, a referral to a point of contact should be made.

Not surprisingly, students with ASD often struggle with the rules about
social interactions when it comes to dating. They sometimes require special-
ized coaching in dating. This coaching can come from campus professionals,
support groups, peers, and role-play situations. Television series that display
scenes of appropriate dating etiquette can be used in role-play teaching situations.

College students with ASD have the same desires to date as most college
students. The everyday stress of college will be difficult for students with
ASD to handle, so adding the stress of dating to their already busy lives can

be overwhelming. Faculty and staff must take their unique needs into consideration and attempt to assist them in finding a balance between their studies and their dating desires.

Students with ASD may or may not have a desire to develop relationships with others while attending college. They will require assistance from their families, faculty, and staff in finding a balance between doing what they enjoy and developing relationships with others. Students with ASD who have positive support systems that encourage developing relationships typically have positive outcomes in college.

CHAPTER HIGHLIGHTS

- Faculty must be supportive and understanding toward the unique needs and demands of individuals with ASD.
- Administration can support faculty by developing letters and fact sheets that share important information pertaining to educating these students.
- Adolescents and adults with ASD are usually interested in friendships, sexual relationships, and marriage.

PONDER AND WONDER

1. Developing relationships can be difficult for individuals with ASD. What types of supports can be put into place on your campus to ensure that students with ASD are developing positive relationships?
2. Explain how you will handle families who do not understand that their family member does not require the same type of support in college as they did while still in high school.
3. Design an information sheet for faculty and staff containing basic information they need to know about students with ASD.

VOICES OF SUCCESS

Paris shared the following:

> The largest obstacle for me to overcome has been that I just get really involved in studying in school, especially as an undergrad. All I cared about was my schoolwork and my grades and getting into medical school, and I let a lot of things like relationships with other people or friendships go by the wayside. Just because at first I didn't realize that a lot of this is reciprocal and just how much it means to my friends if I go to their play, or if I show up at their game, or go hear their thesis defense.
>
> I figured that out eventually. I think that was kind of a big social obstacle to overcome. I was like, "Yeah it is okay to take a break from studying for half

an hour and go do this for your friends, even if it eats up a part of your day or whatever." That was really rewarding when I figured that out, and my friends definitely enjoy it too.

While discussing developing relationships, Conrad remarked:

My first year in college, I was involved with the video yearbook and a martial arts club. My second year in college, I was only participating in two things. I was in a fraternity, and I was a Residential Assistant. After the first years in college, I did not continue to be in any other clubs or organizations, simply because I did not have time for them. I enjoyed trying to hang out with friends, going to the movies, and seeing family. I didn't really have a lot of free time during college. I always worked. Just kind of, like, stupid little part-time jobs that didn't really mean anything.

Chapter Eight

Personal Independence

Leone was diagnosed with High-Functioning Autism (HFA) at four. When his mother took him to enroll in kindergarten, an administrator told her that Leone would only be able to earn a certificate of attendance. Because of his disability, he would not be able to earn a "real" diploma. Leone's parents kept him in that school through first grade, and then they made the decision to homeschool him. Leone became a National Merit Scholar, and he is currently enrolled in the honor's program at a nationally ranked university, where most of his tuition is paid with scholarships.

PARENTS' ROLE IN DEVELOPING INDEPENDENCE

After a child is diagnosed with an Autism Spectrum Disorder, parents will often be overwhelmed with information from multiple sources. Medical professionals, educators, the Internet, friends, and family will provide parents of newly diagnosed children facts, stories, and other information that may confuse parents as they are attempting to process the fact that their child has a developmental disorder.

Will that child be able to graduate from high school? Will he be able to go to college and have a job? Will he ever be able to live independently? These are all questions that parents of children with ASD raise when they receive that diagnosis.

The invisible bubble. One of the most important decisions that these parents will make will be one they may not be aware they are making. When a child receives the ASD diagnosis, some parents put them in an invisible bubble, where the child stays sheltered and dependent on their parents as they age. For many of these children, adulthood is difficult because they have not gained the skills needed to live independently.

Leone's parents could have easily put him in the invisible bubble. They could have followed the recommendations of the school administrator. Would he have learned the skills he needed to go to a university multiple states away from his home?

As normal as possible. Other parents make the decision to treat their child as one without a disability. They may not know what the future holds for their child; however, they want her to be as independent as possible. They are aware that their child has differences, but they include them in activities with their nondisabled peers, even when these activities are difficult and awkward.

They take their child to restaurants, church, shopping, and other public establishments. There may be times when their child throws tantrums in public, where he or she is not able to be consoled. Strangers may stare. However, these parents will continue taking their child out in the public. These parents have high expectations for their child. Jimmy recounted his parents' expectations:

> I've always been told to shoot for the stars, and you can still make the moon. The expectation was always high, and even though I was special, as in Special Ed., and even though I had Asperger's and all this stuff.
>
> My parents expected the same out of me. In fact, probably they expected in some ways, my mom would say no, they expected more out of me than even my brother who wasn't, didn't have a disability. Because now the expectations were always high by everyone, and it was my parents across the board, the expectations were Jimmy is going to go to college. Jimmy is going to go get a job. Jimmy is going to live on his own. From day one, that was the expectation.

Having high expectations for children should come natural for families; however, families of children with ASD will need planning, knowledge, and support for their expectations to become reality. Parents will need to access supports because the journey may hit many bumps along the road. The following are some suggested supports parents can access:

- Parent support groups
- Community groups
- Agency supports
- School personnel
- Medical professionals
- Family
- Friends.

RESPONSIBILITY

Learning how to be responsible is part of growing up. Some children can simply see what their parents and older siblings model, while other children need direct instruction in developing skills to understand and demonstrate personal responsibility. The skills should be taught at the appropriate developmental age of the child. For example, requiring a five-year-old to balance a bank account would probably not be appropriate.

Independent living skills. For individuals to care for themselves, they will need to learn the skills needed to care for themselves. These are not skills that should all be taught when a student reaches high school. Many of the tasks can start in elementary school and before. The more practice the individual gets, the better skilled he becomes.

Household chores. Cooking, cleaning, vacuuming, laundry, yard work . . . the list of household chores goes on and on. Just as their nondisabled peers, individuals with ASD need to learn how to complete household chores. Parents can teach these skills as their child ages. For example, Joe remembered picking up his toys as one of his first household chores.

On the other hand, Jimmy did not start learning to cook until he was in high school; however, he had several chores:

> My responsibilities were garbage. I always did that one. I'd take out the garbage and take the can to the curb. Uh, dishes, if they ask me, my room, and I think I'd clean my bath, I clean my bathroom every once in a while, my mum told me. Those were my big ones.

Children may need direct, repeated instruction in these skills. Sensory difficulties may deter children from some tasks, but parents may find accommodations to make them more tolerable. For example, if the sound of the vacuum is too loud, the individual may wear headphones or earplugs. Smells from certain cleaning products may be unpleasant, so individuals may need to try multiple brands and scents to find one they can tolerate.

Depending on the person, organizational skills may look very different. For example, Elliott describes his organization skills:

> I have my own system, and I do good at that system. I notice immediately when something's been moved or . . . I don't even have to look at the itemizing, just walk into to my room, like, "Who messed with my room?" Like, all this junk here, I know what's in that pile. I know what's in this pile.

Greg, who stated that he had also been diagnosed with Obsessive-Compulsive Disorder (OCD), described his organization skills. He stated, "I'm really organized. I remember having a fit when my mom used to clean my room and put stuff away in, uh, different places. So I like everything where I can find it and I know it's there."

Hygiene. For many, hygiene may seem like a simple skill that should not be a problem to learn. However, for individuals with ASD, who have sensory issues, there are some tasks that may be difficult. Jimmy recalls a specific task with which he struggles:

> I have to force myself to brush my teeth. I hate it, very uncomfortable. I dislike it tremendously. Still, I do it every day just because I have to, but I hate it, hate it, hate it, hate it. Actually I have to buy special toothpaste that's orange flavor because I hate mint toothpaste so much.

Smells, such as in deodorant, soap, or detergent, can be difficult for some individuals with ASD. They may not be aware of their own body odor. Haircuts and shaving are also tasks that may be difficult.

Those with sensory difficulties need support to become more tolerant of some of these sensory stressors. Like Jimmy, they may need to go through multiple trial-and-error attempts to make the task more tolerable. Although he still hates brushing his teeth, he was able to find a flavor of toothpaste that he can tolerate to get it done each day.

Poor hygiene can hinder an individual socially, and it can also keep a person from gaining employment. Although accommodations can be made to attire, a person needs to be clean. Charts, schedules, and pictures may need to be provided for a person with ASD to complete their daily hygiene routines.

Budget. Managing money can be a difficult task for individuals with and without disabilities, but it is a skill that individuals need to be able to provide for themselves. Children can be taught the value of money at an early age by opening a savings account. Parents can bring their child shopping and give them a set amount of money and a list of items to purchase. Ordering at a restaurant is another way that children can practice their money skills.

Individuals should practice budgeting skills before attempting to live independently. Having a child earn an allowance and practice saving and spending is a great way to practice with money. Using spreadsheets and other types of programs is another way for individuals to practice budgeting skills.

Transportation. The ability to drive provides an individual with a great sense of freedom, such as Elliott described in chapter 3; however, not all people are able to drive. Individuals who cannot drive need to develop a plan for getting around. Will they use public transportation? What will they do if public transportation is not available where they live? Are there taxis available? Can a bicycle be used?

Parents and the individual will need to investigate the available transportation methods in their area. They may need to seek assistance from agencies, such as the Department of Assistive and Rehabilitative Services (DARS), who will sometimes pay for transportation for disabled individuals to get to work or college. Once a plan is developed, the individual will need to practice the mode of transportation, just like someone who is driving to a location for the first time.

CHAPTER HIGHLIGHTS

- Parents must avoid the bubble of shelter and dependence.
- Families of those with ASD need to access supports.
- Start teaching independent living skills early.

PONDER AND WONDER

1. What type(s) of support could your campus offer to parents of children with ASD?
2. If you saw a parent putting their child with ASD in the invisible bubble of shelter and dependence, would you address it? If so, how?
3. If you had a student who was having difficulty with personal hygiene, how would you address it?

VOICES OF SUCCESS

Elliott, a college freshman, shared his parents' thoughts on his independence, particularly driving. "They're glad that I'm doing that, but still it's . . . they're like, Okay. What do we do now? Now you don't need us." Elliott explained what helped him make the decision to go to college:

> I guess time, really. Just finally realizing who cares. I mean, your fears are really not that important when it comes to the grand scheme of things. If you keep sheltering yourself, you're not going to get anywhere.
>
> My mom is, I guess you could say, she was the perfect example of being shy and letting the shyness get the best of her and not taking the opportunities that were arise, arose to her because of her shyness. My dad also would say that you have to break through your fears of not liking this and just, just do it because it's better in the long run to say, "It's not important." Just break through it.

Olivier suggested some strategies he felt students with HFA or AS could implement in higher education. He mentioned the following:

> One of the things I could do is get out more. Be around different people instead of just around people in my major. That is basically who I talk to. I do talk to orchestra members, but there are other people in the college world who

I could befriend as well. Another way of doing it is actually doing my work to the fullest rather than doing the bare minimum, which is what I did last year.

Colleges should allow autistic kids to join things. I know that in, especially a liberal school, they like to have everybody involved because they are all about equality. One of the things they could do is say, hey come along and join us and not just push them off to the side discriminate against them. Just say everybody is allowed to be here, everybody is allowed to hear this.

Chapter Nine

Strategies That Work

Strategies for college students with ASD will assist them in becoming self-sufficient individuals. ASD students are encouraged to consistently use selective strategies to accomplish given tasks. This will enable them to gain a sense of pride and independence. This chapter provides strategies for ASD students who are striving to achieve success during their years in higher education.

KNOWLEDGE IS POWER

The more individuals with ASD know about themselves, the better. When they make the transition to college, they must be their own advocate, because they will be required to communicate their needs in order to receive appropriate services and accommodations.

Disability. Individuals with disabilities need to have a true understanding of their disability and how it affects them. No two people with ASD are the same, so it is important for individuals to know how their disability affects their life. Ideally, an individual is diagnosed early in life, so he or she can have an explanation for his or her behavior as he grows. Elliott explained how his parents told him about his diagnosis:

> They told me little bits at a time. When they knew I could comprehend what was being said. So about a little, every little bit at a time, like, "It's this. It does this." As problems arised, and I didn't understand them, they would tell me.

Some people are not diagnosed early, or they may have been diagnosed incorrectly before receiving their diagnosis of ASD. Abigail, who was not diagnosed until she was forty-one, which was ten years after her son was diagnosed, had an idea that she had an ASD. She explained her feelings with her diagnosis. "Now that I know I have autism, I understand how my core features express themselves differently. Now I get it."

Social effects. Individuals with ASD often have difficulties with social interactions, including making eye contact, initiating conversation, and understanding personal space, just to name a few. Individuals need to know how their disability affects them socially so they can learn and make adjustments. Social skills development is an ongoing learning process. Abigail explained her process to address social difficulties that have come up during board meetings:

> When that happens that's an occasion whereby, um, nobody would have seen it as a disability. They may have seen it as a character flaw or personality issue, but they would not have seen it as a disability and they still don't. You know, I have to call attention to it and frame it for them for people to see it as part of my condition.
>
> So, like if I'm . . . national board meeting and I want to express something but I don't know that I can do it effectively without making someone mad, I'll just say, you know, I'm really not sure how to say this, but I'm just going to put it out there, and you know, recognize that this is a, kind of, unfiltered response but here's how I feel.

Joe reported that when he moved onto his university campus, he wanted to be the big man on campus and make friends with everyone he came in contact with. He recognized that that was not the best way to go about meeting people, so he has had to make some changes in his behavior. None of his friends went to the same university that he had gone to, but he joined a club baseball team, and he's hoping to meet some friends through it.

Academic effects. Some students with ASD have difficulty with academics. Although they may be highly intelligent, they may struggle with skills such as organization, study skills, time management, and communication. Professors and disabilities office personnel can provide students with strategies to be successful. Students may need to access writing centers or other tutorial services to gain more support.

Learning style. College students are responsible for their learning, so they need to have an understanding of their learning style. They will need to be able to answer the following questions:

- How do they learn the best? (Example: visual, auditory, kinesthetic learner)
- What is the best environment for learning? (Example: quiet library, bedroom with the radio, etc.)
- Would online classes be better than in-person classes?

Accommodations. College students with disabilities can receive accommodations in higher education; however, they must seek out the services. In order to do that, they will need to meet with the Office of Disabilities at their institution to investigate services. Those with ASD often receive accommodations in elementary and secondary school. During this time, they need to identify what accommodations are beneficial to them. Some of the following accommodations are helpful and available to students:

- Alternative testing environment
- Copy of class notes
- Extended time on writing assignments
- Technology usage or assistance.

The main thing for students to remember is that accommodations should be appropriate for the individual needs of the student. Not all accommodations work for everyone.

Identify and access support systems. Identifying support systems is critical to success in higher education. Support systems will prove to be a remarkable way to stay in touch with those who can help students with ASD and to have knowledge of available programs. Support systems should be identified during the transition from high school to college and be reviewed on an annual basis.

Students with ASD should identify support systems at home, school, and in the community. Faculty can assist these students in identifying their support systems by working hand in hand with these support systems to provide the best opportunities for success. Students with ASD have input into the amount of participation faculty and staff can have with support systems, so permission to contact or talk to these support systems will be required.

Home support. For many students with ASD, support from home will be easy to find. Their success is often a result of a strong support system at home. Faculty and staff can assist students with ASD in identifying support from home by having them list the things for which they can rely on their family for support.

Identifying home supports does not have to take place on the college level. Ideally, the students will come with an idea of the supports they can find from home. These supports may be as simple as daily phone calls or text messages letting the family know how things are going, or as complex as weekly visits to/from home to ensure the student is functioning well in college.

Wolf, Brown, and Bork et al. (2009) suggested that families share the following information with the faculty and staff:

- Routines and interests

- Likes and dislikes
- Previous school experiences
- Relationships with peers
- Relationships with teachers
- Types of support services received in the past
- Challenges and/or problems (especially psychiatric).

It is important to remember that parents are accustomed to being the primary contact for their child's educational needs. Now that their child is considered an adult, he must be encouraged to foster independence as much as possible. Discussions about fostering independence with parents can prove to be helpful to all parties involved.

Academic support. Identifying and accessing supports on an academic level is very important for students with ASD. Some students with ASD do not have academic needs in the area of the subject matter, but most will have academic needs in the area of accommodations, such as social skills. These needs can easily be met on campus as long as the student is aware of services available.

Accessing disability support services is often the first step in identifying and accessing academic support. All students with ASD should make an appointment and visit the Office of Disability Support on their campus. Even if they do not require academic support, this office can be a wonderful place to find information on other types of campus support.

Some campuses have support groups or social skills groups designed specifically for students with ASD. Faculty and staff can assist students with ASD in accessing these services by providing information about these services to all students and families upon registration and orientation prior to the start of each semester.

Students can also find academic support through their peers. It is important to encourage them to participate in study groups and tutoring programs offered by their peers. Information regarding these supports can be disseminated through the Office of Disability Support, faculty, and even through dorm information centers.

Students with ASD should be encouraged to be as explicit as possible when asking for academic support (Harpur, Lawlor, and Fitzgerald, 2004). These students need to be taught to state exactly what they need and why they need it. If faculty and staff are not properly trained in the basics of ASD, it will be difficult for them to decipher what the student needs without explicit information.

Community support. While it is not required, identifying community support can really be helpful for students with ASD. Faculty and staff can assist students with ASD in identifying community support by making professional connections with these organizations. Most organizations would be happy to assist college personnel in promoting their services.

Scheduling times for community services to come onto campus and promote their services would be beneficial to faculty, staff, and students. Promotion can be as easy as setting up an information booth in the student center. If there is an abundance of community supports for students with ASD in the area, campus administration can schedule a community fair and invite all agencies in the area.

Keeping community service organizations involved on campus will bridge the gap between the community and campus. Seeing community organizations on campus may increase the comfort level for students, faculty, and staff. Campuses and community organizations that work together will provide a more seamless approach to helping students with ASD.

PERSONALIZED STRATEGIES FOR ASD STUDENTS

Learning and instructional strategies are selected according to the needs of an individual student. Students should be encouraged to use strategies that will aid them in the areas of scheduling, organization, and communication.

Scheduling. The following is a review of scheduling strategies that will assist ASD students in higher education:

- ASD students should use monthly calendars, either paper or electronic format.
- Electronic devices such as cell phones, laptops, and desktop computers can also be used in planning schedules.
- Students should list all course requirements in writing, including assignment due dates and test dates.

Paris discussed that students with HFA or AS should find strategies that work for them and pursue their academics to the best of their ability. She recommended developing time-management strategies such as a schedule that plans out every part of the day, setting reminders from that schedule, or having a friend text to remind you of important events and timelines.

Organization. Students with ASD need organizational strategies to assist with time management in classes and to function daily. Organizing assignments and schedules will assist students in a higher-education setting. The following is a review of strategies, which were mentioned in chapter 6:

- ASD students should create a quiet space to study and arrange study materials so they are readily available during study sessions.

- Checklists should also be used, which will serve as a visual aid for the ASD student.
- Binders and electronic portfolios can be used for maintaining course notes, handouts, and syllabi.
- Class assignments and projects should be broken down into chunks, which will allow students to work on sections at a time until the completion of the assigned task.

While discussing time management with Elliott, he laughed as he described the following organizational skills:

> My mess, messiness, and being unorganized is my weakness at home. I guess I just stick to my rules that I print for myself at home. I mean, I, I have things I put in certain areas. I have my own system, and I do good at that system. I notice immediately when something's been moved or I don't even have to look at the itemizing, just walk into my room, like, "Who messed with my room?" Like, all this junk here, I know what's in that pile. I know what's in this pile. I just memorize the room, so I just have to walk in and be like, "What happened to that penny?"

Communication. ASD students have problems communicating and understanding personal space. They have difficulty interpreting words with double meanings. The use of sarcasm and metaphors are also difficult for them to comprehend. ASD students' conversations are sometimes repetitive. The following strategies are suggested to assist with communication:

- Provide clear directions with step-by-step instructions.
- Provide written information that coincides with verbal lectures.
- Allow ASD students the option to work independently when group assignments are made.
- Provide visuals to facilitate understanding.
- Use laptops for taking notes.
- Ask for clarification on assignments.
- Use recording devices in class when possible.
- Ask for preferential seating.

Joe explained that communication was a big weakness for him. He expressed, "Say, if I wanted to go get milk. I would be able to think that, you know, I would want some milk and stuff. The weakness was communicating that to my parents." Joe remembered that his speech was delayed, but he was provided speech therapy early so he would communicate wants and needs through pictures until he was able to use words.

CHAPTER HIGHLIGHTS

- Higher-education institutions should take steps toward erasing the stigma of having a disability.
- Students with ASD must identify their support systems and needs at home, on campus, and in the community.

PONDER AND WONDER

1. How can higher-education institutions include ASD students in areas of decision making regarding accommodations for students with disabilities?
2. Families are accustomed to being in charge of their children's education. How would you handle a parent who wants to remain in charge, even after their child has started the semester, while remaining sensitive to the unique needs of this student with ASD?

VOICES OF SUCCESS

Conrad recommended that higher-education institutions provide professors with educational opportunities to learn more about students with AS. He recommended these educational opportunities address how to deal with students with AS and also ways in which they can help these students.

Paris indicated that she felt higher-education institutions could be more forthcoming about the services they provide to individuals with HFA or AS. She recommended being more open about the disability so that others would be more accepting of individuals with HFA or AS. Paris recommended higher-education institutions take steps toward erasing the stigma of having a disability.

Russell discussed the experiences he had while attending college that have helped him to be successful in the pursuit of his degree. He described these experiences:

> Well, for them to help me, to help them, I kind of get to know them better, kind of make a friend with them. Basically, you get to know the teacher a little better, and they understand your needs much better. Sometimes just humor them, and, you know, just basically act. You know, be a little individualistic unlike the other students who usually just tend to put their heads down and just kind of groan a lot. I sometimes ask professors for extended time.

Chapter Ten

College Preparation

Going to college takes a great deal of preparation and planning for all students. For students with ASD, the planning is usually more involved. According to Roberts (2010), postsecondary education is a viable option for many individuals with ASD, but it entails a great deal of planning and support to aid the student.

Planning for the ASD student must be individualized and based on the student's particular needs. Numerous questions need to be answered before the student can enter their higher-education program. Some questions include:

- What type of program will be most appropriate for the student? Face to face, online?
- Will the student commute or live on campus? Will he or she need accommodations for living? Will the student require transportation?
- What level of support will the student need? What accommodations will he or she need for instruction, if any?

CHOOSING THE INSTITUTION

Students entering higher education have a multitude of options that will meet their individual needs in order to reach their postsecondary employment goals. Four-year universities, community colleges, and technical schools offer programs that can be tailored to meet the needs of full-time and part-time students. The multiple options are particularly beneficial for students with ASD.

Program. Will the student be interested in a four-year degree? Is the student interested in a certificate program? If the student with ASD receives special education services, then he or she will be provided transition services to help determine postsecondary employment and education goals. Determining the appropriate program for the student is individualized and based on the needs and goals of the student.

Four-year colleges and universities. Public and private universities, liberal arts colleges, and career-specific colleges that offer bachelor's degrees are all considered four-year colleges or universities. These schools offer degree programs that typically take up to four years or more to complete and result in a bachelor's degree.

Class sizes can range from small to very large, depending on the college or university size. These schools have an acceptance process that often includes ACT or SAT scores, high school GPA, and a lengthy application process.

Many of these four-year colleges or universities also offer master's degrees through graduate schools. Some students will begin their higher-education journey attending a community college, then transfer to a four-year college or university. Accommodations are available for students who have a documented disability; however, the student must seek out those services on their own.

Community college. Community colleges are a great place for students to start their higher education. These institutions are usually open enrollment, which means that the student does not have to take SAT or ACT tests; however, they will often have to take placement tests to determine the classes they should take.

Class sizes are smaller than those found on large university campuses, and both academic and technical programs are provided. Some students will earn two-year associate degrees at the community college, and others will use the credits they earn to transfer to a four-year university. Other students will complete certificate programs that will prepare them for specific jobs, without earning a degree.

Many students, including those with ASD, choose community colleges to begin their higher-education journey because it is a better transition for them. It is higher education on a smaller scale. Accommodations are available for students who have a documented disability, and the student must seek out those services.

Technical school. Technical schools are another option for students. These institutions are also open enrollment, and students can earn two-year degrees, certificates, or credits that transfer to other institutions. Technical schools offer programs that are technical in nature, such as welding, automotive technology, computer technology, medical technology, and other technical programs. These programs are more hands-on, where students gain practical knowledge along with the theoretical knowledge. Accommodations are also available for students who have a documented disability, and the students must seek out those services.

Location. Deciding on a location is an important decision for students with ASD. Will the student attend a local college, which will allow commuting from home? Will the student attend a local college and live on campus? Will the student attend a college out of town or out of state? These are all options for students, including online higher-education programs.

Commuting. Commuting is a popular option for many students. Students can live at home and travel back and forth to campus. For students with ASD, this can be a great choice because they can attend school and remain in the comfort of their known surroundings. Routine is very important for individuals with ASD. This option would benefit those who need their established supports readily available.

Living on campus. Living on campus is another option for students, whether they live within commuting distance or multiple states from home. Dorm life provides students with social activities. Students with ASD may find living on campus helpful since they often have difficulty accessing and navigating social situations.

Ackles, Fields, and Skinner (2013) reported that even though individuals with ASD often have strong cognitive abilities, their social impairments and communication skill deficits might negatively impact their residential living experience. The researchers added that residential living can be complicated for this population of students because there are several adjustments that students make to campus living, such as organization, building peer relationships, independent living, and shared living quarters.

For individuals who often have a lack of friends and social supports beyond their family, campus living can be overwhelming (Cohen, 2011). Thus, the Disability Services Office becomes the primary resource for students with disabilities (Dente & Coles, 2012). Students with documented disabilities can receive accommodations in higher education, which includes accommodations to their on-campus living arrangements. Of course, accommodations are based on the individual needs of the student and availability.

Single rooms are an example of an accommodation that is often available for students with a documented disability. Some students with ASD will find this accommodation to be a necessity. Lighting is another accommodation that may be available. Some students with ASD have a level of sensitivity to lights.

Instructional delivery. Gone are the days of students only being able to access college programs through traditional, face-to-face instruction. There are now several program options for students, which are particularly beneficial to those on the autism spectrum.

Face-to-face instruction. Traditional, face-to-face classes are classes that meet one or multiple times per week on campus. These types of classes can sometimes be difficult for students on the autism spectrum. Professors may require students to participate in group projects, and students with ASD may lack the social skills required to appropriately participate in the group. Since communication is also usually an area of weakness for students on the spectrum, participating in class discussions may also be a struggle.

Online learning. Online learning is rapidly growing as the choice for many college students. Students find the flexibility of online learning to be appealing, especially for those students who work and have families.

Many students with ASD prefer taking classes online. The courses are very structured, which students find beneficial. Students can also avoid awkward social situations, such as group projects and other activities. Communication, which is also an area of difficulty for many on the autism spectrum, is often easier via the online learning process. Most communication occurs through electronic means.

On the other hand, students with ASD may find online classes to be challenging because they are more in charge of their learning. Organization skills, along with time-management skills and motivation, are imperative to the online learner. Students will also need to access supports if they have any difficulty with the class.

DETERMINING THE LEVEL OF SUPPORT

ASD affects each individual differently. They all have different needs, and there is no blanket accommodation or support that meets the needs of everyone. When planning to enter higher education, it is crucial that the needs of the individual are assessed and a plan is developed.

Some students with ASD will require very little support in higher education. They may choose to not disclose their disability to professors or seek services or accommodations. These students are successful without any added supports.

Other students may require accommodations to be successful in higher education. Accommodations in college are usually minimal, and the purpose is to not provide students with an advantage over other students. Copies of class notes, alternative testing environments, interpreters, assistive technology, and extended time are just a few accommodations that may be available to students. If a student needs accommodations, he or she will need to seek the services by meeting with the student services department at their institution.

There are some students who require more support than allowed with accommodations. In fact, some parents will hire a liaison to mediate between the student and school personnel. In some cases, parents will follow their child to college and provide support for him or her.

MAKING THE TRANSITION

In order for students to make a successful transition to college life, planning needs to occur. Students should participate in activities prior to the start of classes so they can become more familiar with the campus and supports that are available.

Orientation. Institutions in higher education typically provide orientation for incoming freshmen and transfer students. These orientations are usually a couple of days in length, which provide time for students to learn about the institution, including traditions, and also have the opportunity to meet other incoming freshmen and form relationships. Some institutions offer early arrival programs and extended orientation programs because they are aware that some students need more time and support to make the transition to higher education.

Hughes (2009) suggested that before students with ASD actually begin classes, they need to participate in orientation and tour the campus to learn where important points of interest are, specifically the Disability Office, so they can know where to go for help. Thus, students should participate in early arrival programs (Ackles, Fields, & Skinner, 2013). Students with ASD need to take advantage of these programs when they are available.

Transportation. A decision college students need to make when planning for college is the method of transportation. Will the student drive? What if the disability prohibits the student from being able to drive? These are just a couple of questions that should be asked when planning for transportation for a college student with ASD.

Students that are commuting to college from home may choose to drive. However, some students cannot drive due to their disability. Public transportation is an option, if it is available. Also, adult agencies will sometimes provide transportation for those with disabilities. Carpooling with a peer is another option for students. Family members oftentimes provide transportation for ASD students.

Students who live on campus may or may not choose to bring a car with them. Although Leone had earned a driver's license in his home state, he and his family opted for him to not take a car with him to college. Instead, he used public transportation and a bicycle. Universities will also provide transportation to shopping areas, such as malls or grocery stores, so students have the opportunity to pick up necessities.

CHAPTER HIGHLIGHTS

- Planning for the ASD student should be individualized and based on the student's particular needs.

- Students entering higher education have a multitude of options that will meet their individual needs in order to reach their postsecondary employment goals. Four-year universities, community colleges, and technical schools offer programs that can be tailored to meet the needs of full-time and part-time students. The multiple options are particularly beneficial for students with ASD.
- Deciding on a location is an important decision for students with ASD.
- Students should participate in activities prior to the start of classes so they can become more familiar with the campus and supports that are available.

PONDER AND WONDER

1. What online resources can higher-education institutions provide to assist ASD students who are planning for college?
2. What specific activities should be planned for ASD students during orientation, without bringing attention to their disability?

VOICES OF SUCCESS

Leone was entering a large, nationally ranked university multiple states from his home. His mother recognized that he would need support to make the transition to university life a successful experience, especially since he would be so far from home. Leone's mother chose to come with him several weeks before classes started. She lived in a hotel in the area for several weeks, and she worked with him to get him adjusted to his new surroundings.

Murphy offered recommendations to other students with HFA or AS. She suggested the following:

Well, I have offered my advice online sometimes when people have problems. I do try to kind of say that you can bring in or you can have your doctor or psychiatrist even talk to them if worse comes to worst or get the campus psych involved or something. If it is really a big issue, don't be afraid to bring in information about what you have because the biggest problem I noticed in the entire autism community is that there is so much misinformation about what autism actually is. Which is why I am so reluctant in real life to say I am autistic.

People would think I am like mentally retarded, and I would say they are completely different. I am socially retarded. I am definitely mentally there socially, I don't know. It [autism] is completely different. I mean there is just so much. There is no look for autism except for maybe wearing the same clothes for five days in a row. I don't know a lot of people do that. It is like very tough.

The best advice I can give to people is to try to spread the correct information and do it in a way that shows that one person with autism is just one person with autism and that we are not a box of chocolate soldiers. We are actually all different, and that it is a spectrum there are people on one end or the other and in the middle. It is getting the correct information out there. It is one of the reasons I blog is because there is so much misinformation.

I like to share what I actually do have problems with and what I do well. Then I can talk to other people on the spectrum who have similar problems, and we work together and all that. For me, my problems are usually solved by spreading some information. I think the biggest thing you can do if you are having a problem with somebody is share with them exactly what is going on. Let them know what is actually happening and mostly they will be more sympathetic. You always get those like horrible people who don't.

Best thing I did was actually follow exactly what I wanted to do and go into my field. When I went into my field I found a lot of people like me. It was huge for me because it was nice to know that there were other people that were interested in preserving history the way I was interested in it. My Internet friends were great because they actually shared my interest and didn't judge me. If you are having trouble making friends, do not be afraid to turn to the Internet.

I mean I have met some of my online friends in real life, and it has been wonderful and very exciting to actually meet up. So again really do not be afraid to turn to that because sometimes that can be some of your best friends as amazing as that sounds.

If your campus does have a support group, I would highly recommend it. Mine did not because my college was like about the size of this room. There is no shame in going to a therapist and getting advice from the therapist. I find a lot of people are very ashamed to go get mental health and there really should be no shame in it.

I am so open about my experience with my therapist online because I wish people would see that there is nothing to fear. If anyone is judging you for it, don't listen to them. I mean you are doing something for yourself. You are helping getting yourself to a more healthy place for you and it doesn't matter what they think.

Again, I would have loved the support group so much because I would have really loved the opportunity to make more friends on the spectrum. It would have probably helped a lot to, I think, improve our college experiences because we could of all helped each other through that. I am sure some schools do it. I wish more schools would do this or just any sort of group therapy would have been great because I think it would have been nice to voice my issue, voice my grievances somewhere and really find some support.

My roommate was going through a lot of problems of her own and she was not exactly the best sounding board, so I would have really loved to have some people who I could of really just sounded off with and really been in a no judgment zone.

My campus psychiatrist was a lifesaver. I loved her. I definitely would not have been able to do it without her. She was somebody I could talk to and share things, and I felt like I was in a place where I was not being judged and I was safe.

If you have an on campus psych, that is a great person to turn to. They are usually very good at what they do and they are there to comfort you and help you through. They counsel you along and give you advice. They are wonderful and if you are in a situation where you are working as a research assistant and if a professor really takes you under their wing they can be a valuable mentor, especially if you feel safe with them. If you open up to them, that is always a good thing as well.

Finding trusting adults is really helpful because some of the time a lot of people in our age group don't understand what is going on and of course a lot of adults don't understand what is going on. As I said before, do not be afraid to reach out to the Internet because sometimes that is where the most understanding people are. If they are not near you, still talk to them as if they would be there.

Definitely do it, that's what I would tell others. I was so happy that I did because I really feel like I found myself in college. I went out of high school thinking I knew who I was and what I wanted to do, but when I went to college I really came into my own. Especially after I had the diagnosis and I knew what I was up against. After I graduated, I really started to feel like I could do this. I realized through college that I actually can function as a human outside of the home.

I was four hours away from home, and that was tough. I would probably tell them to go away if it is their thing. I mean you can also stay close to home especially if you have a good working relationship with your therapist or if you feel safer with your parents you can commute. Grad school especially has been the best experience for me because in grad school I really feel confident for the first time in my life. I actually feel very confident in who I am as a person and I think I have gotten that because I have done fairly well in grad school so far.

I really feel like I am accomplishing something in my life and when they hand you that expensive piece of paper at the end of the little thing; I got my piece of expensive paper on the wall. It's very nice to be handed that piece of paper for four years of hard work.

College is not for everybody; there are some people that don't particularly want to go to school or feel like school is the right path for them and that is fine, but if you are considering college, want to go to college, don't be afraid to do it. It is absolutely wonderful and eventually if you do happen to very luckily find the right friends on campus they will be your friends for life. You live together and they kind of become like an extended family on campus.

It is definitely worth doing, worth taking that risk. It's a big step. I mean if you go to a school that doesn't have the support that you need, that is going to steer you right towards a breakdown, and nobody needs that. I wish they were a little more open about what they are providing. I know they always mention disability services off on the side.

It is usually more implied that it is for physical disabilities and for ADHD. Those are the two that are mostly talked about. They don't talk much about autism; that is usually brushed under the rug a lot and that is not really helpful. So that is probably why I didn't think about going to my disabilities services as an undergrad because I didn't even know they were there. They don't really talk about it much.

I wish it was a thing that was more publicized because so many people do live with mental health issues. I definitely have social anxiety as a result of how I was treated growing up by my peers. Things like that I would like to know when I am going to a school that these services are available to me. I would like to know before I go there for a campus tour.

I would like to be a little more prominent because I know there is a stigma on disability, and it's always going to be there to some extent. I would like it to be more of an accepted thing, and I think colleges could take a good step in making it a more accepted thing by just showing that disabilities services are nothing to be ashamed of and that having them is nothing to be ashamed of.

My family was absolutely incredible, so be like my parents! One of the most important things you can do as a parent is be supportive of your kid and let them feel things out. Let them experiment and see what works for them and let them find out who they want to be. That is the nice thing about college because you get to start over and really establish yourself as who you want to be. It took me awhile to really establish who I was, and college really helped me.

If I look at my writing samples for four years, it just shows a complete difference in the language I used in my more causal writing. I have changed so much. I know a lot of that was in just finding myself more and growing myself more as a person. If you let your kid go, if you let your special needs child go to school and just make sure you support them, and if they need you try to be there to the best of your ability. I definitely had quite a few phone calls to my parents.

I wish colleges would offer therapy animals because that is another thing that really helps. That helps everybody, not just spectrum people or people with mental health issues. It helps everybody to have like it is finals week you want to go pet a dog, it helps a lot. I know for some special needs students, it is allowed.

I guess for parents the most important thing you can do is be supportive and do your best to be there for your child when they need you. They will need you at some point. They may not want to admit it now when they are going off to school, but they will need you and they will mature into realizing that they do need you.

Weblinks

The Internet is a great place to access information and resources to help individuals with autism spectrum disorders and their families find supports and guidance with their planning. The amount of information can be overwhelming. Our participants mentioned the following beneficial sites. This is not an all-encompassing list, but it is a great start.

10 Impressive College Programs for Students with Autism

> Provides information on programs for college students with autism.
> http://www.bestcollegesonline.com/blog/2011/05/25/10-impressive-special-college-programs-for-students-with-autism/

Achieving in Higher Education with Autism and Developmental Disabilities (AHEADD)

> Complements traditional college accommodations by providing coaching and mentoring support to improve social interactions, self-advocacy, organizational skills, and communication.
> http://www.aheadd.org/

Association on Higher Education and Disability (AHEAD)

> Addresses the needs of students with disabilities in higher education.
> http://www.ahead.org

Autism Society

> Exists to improve the lives of all affected by autism by increasing public awareness about the day-to-day issues faced by people on the spectrum, advocating for appropriate services for individuals across the

lifespan, and providing the latest information regarding treatment, education, research, and advocacy.
http://www.autism-society.org/

Autism Speaks

An advocacy organization dedicated to funding research into the causes, prevention, treatments, and a cure for autism; increasing awareness of autism spectrum disorders; and advocating for the needs of individuals with autism and their families.
https://www.autismspeaks.org/family-services/resource-library/post-secondary-education-resources

Disabilities, Opportunities, Internetworking, and Technology (DO-IT) Center

The DO-IT Center is dedicated to empowering people with disabilities through technology and education. It promotes awareness and accessibility—in both the classroom and the workplace—to maximize the potential of individuals with disabilities and to make our communities more vibrant, diverse, and inclusive.
https://www.washington.edu/doit/preparing-college-online-tutorial

Fast Facts for Faculty—Universal Design for Learning

Provides strategies for faculty to assist students.
http://ada.osu.edu/resources/fastfacts/

I'm Determined

Provides information and resources to parents, educators, and students on developing self-determination skills.
http://www.imdetermined.org

National Technical Assistance Center on Transition

Resources for transition planning.
http://www.nsttac.org

University Students with Autism and Asperger's Syndrome Website

Article and resources.
http://www.cns.dircon.co.uk/index.html

US Autism & Asperger Association

Establishes standards for Autism and Asperger Syndrome training, and aligns with local community resources to offer support for the entire a utism and Asperger communities.
http://www.usautism.org/uscap/index.htm

Wrightslaw

Provides legal information for students with disabilities.
http://www.wrightslaw.com

Resources

AUTISM IN COLLEGE FACT SHEET

Autism is defined as significant deficits in social communication, social interactions, and repetitive patterns of behavior. Each student with autism will be affected differently, which will present with different characteristics. Diagnosis of autism often occurs in childhood but sometimes occurs in adulthood.

Students with autism may have:

- trouble with social cues, auditory cues, and conversational language
- issues with transitions and changes in their daily routines
- repetition of body movement or oral phrases that do not pertain to the conversation
- trouble with fine-motor skills, especially handwriting
- issues staying on topic during class conversations due to intense interests
- sensitivity to lights and sounds

In addition, students with autism may be dealing with comorbid conditions such as ADHD, depression, learning disabilities, anxiety, and more. It is important for college personnel to encourage students with autism to access all support services on campus from which they would benefit.

Students with autism are in college because they choose to be there. They want to do just as well as other students in their classes. The difficulties presented, due to autism, oftentimes make it hard to be successful in college. With the right supports, the difficulties can be minimized and the student can find success. The Disability Support Service office can prove to be a beneficial place to start when looking for supports on campus.

TIPS FOR DISCUSSION

Discussion and debate in the classroom can be difficult for students with autism. They often have a difficult time following the conversation and responding appropriately. The following are guidelines that can be shared with students with autism prior to a classroom discussion/debate.

1. **When in agreement with someone/something:**
   I agree with _____ because . . .
   I like what _____ said because . . .
2. **When in disagreement with someone/something:**
   I disagree with _____ because . . .
   I am not sure I agree with what _____ said because . . .
3. **When clarification is needed:**
   Repeat that, please.
   Explain that more.
   What evidence do you have?
4. **When giving confirmation on another idea:**
   I believe . . .
   I think . . .
   I found further evidence of what you said.
5. **When feeling confused:**
   I don't understand _____.
   I am confused about _____.
   I am not clear on _____.
6. **When extending on another person's thought:**
   I was thinking about what _____ said, and I was wondering . . .
   This makes me think _____.

IDENTIFYING SUPPORTS

Students need to know who to go to when they need help. This is particularly important for students with ASD. Supports vary depending on the environment. The following graphics can aid students in identifying their supports in each aspect of their life. Use this graphic organizer to identify supports in the following areas.

At Home

- Family
- Friends
- Neighbors
- Roommates (if living on campus)
- Resident Assistant (if living on campus)

On Campus

- Professors
- Disability Office Counselor
- Classmates
- Advisor
- On-campus Learning Centers
- Tutors
- Library personnel
- Study groups
- Extracurricular interest groups

Community

- Friends
- Community support groups
- Church groups
- Medical professionals
- Agency personnel

DAILY AGENDA

Date _____

DAILY GOAL:

Table 10.1.

TIME	CLASS SCHEDULE	WORK SCHEDULE	PERSONAL SCHEDULE	NOTES
7 AM				
8 AM				
9 AM				
10 AM				
11 AM				
12 PM				
1 PM				
2 PM				
3 PM				
4 PM				
5 PM				
6 PM				
7 PM				
8 PM				
9 PM				

DAILY SUCCESS:

WEEKLY AGENDA

Week of _____

WEEKLY GOAL:

Table 10.2.

TIME	SUN	MON	TUES	WED	THURS	FRI	SAT	NOTES
7 AM								
8 AM								
9 AM								
10 AM								
11 AM								
12 PM								
1 PM								
2 PM								
3 PM								
4 PM								
5 PM								
6 PM								
7 PM								
8 PM								
9 PM								

WEEKLY SUCCESS:

Monthly Calendar
Month_____
Year_____

MONTHLY GOAL:

Table 10.3.

Set four goals for each week
1)
2)
3)
4)
1)
2)
3)
4)
1)
2)
3)
4)
1)
2)
3)
4)
1)
2)
3)
4)

MONTHLY SUCCESS:

References

Ackles, L., Fields, H., & Skinner, R. (2013). A collaborative support model for students on the Autism Spectrum in college and university housing. *Journal of College & University Student Housing, 39/40*(2/1), 200–12.

Adreon, D., & Durocher, J. S. (2007). Evaluating the college transition needs of individuals with high-functioning Autism Spectrum Disorders. *Intervention in School and Clinic, 42*(5).

American Psychiatric Association. (1980). *Diagnostic and Statistical Manual of Mental Disorders* (3rd ed.). Washington, DC: Author.

American Psychiatric Association. (1994). *Diagnostic and Statistical Manual of Mental Disorders* (4th ed.). Washington, DC: Author.

American Psychiatric Association. (2013). *Diagnostic and Statistical Manual of Mental Disorders* (5th ed.). Washington, DC: Author.

Asaro-Saddler, K., & Bak, N. (2014). Persuasive writing and self-regulation training for writers with Autism Spectrum Disorders. *Journal of Special Education, 48*(2), 92–105. doi: 10.1177/0033466912474101

Ball-Erickson, M. (2012). Effective reading comprehension strategies for students with Autism Spectrum Disorders in the elementary general education classroom. Doctoral Dissertation. North Michigan University, MI.

Barnhill, G. P. (2007). Outcomes in adults with Asperger Syndrome. *Focus on Autism & Other Developmental Disabilities, 22*(2), 116–26.

Barnhill, G. P. (2014). Supporting students with Asperger Syndrome on college campuses: Current practices. *Focus on Autism and Other Developmental Disabilities, 1–13.* doi: 10.1177/1088357614523121

Begeer, S., Koot, H., Rieffe, C., Terwogt, M., & Stegge, H. (2008). Emotional competence in children with autism: Diagnostic criteria and empirical evidence. *Developmental Review, 28,* 342–69.

Burton-Hoyle, S. (2011). Autism Spectrum Disorders: Strategies toward a self-determined life for your child. *Exceptional Parent, 41*(4), 26–27.

Camarena, P. M., & Sarigiani, P. A. (2009). Postsecondary educational aspirations of high-functioning adolescents with Autism Spectrum Disorders and their parents. *Focus on Autism and Other Developmental Disabilities, 24*(2), 115–28.

Carter, E. W., Owens, L., Trainor, A. A., Sun, Y., & Sweeden, B. (2009). Self-determination skills and opportunities of adolescents with severe intellectual and developmental disabilities. *American Journal on Intellectual and Developmental Disabilities, 114*(3), 179–92. doi: 10.1352/1944-7558-114.3.179

Case-Smith, J., Weaver, L. L., & Fristad, M. A. (2015). A systematic review of sensory processing interventions for children with Autism Spectrum Disorders. *Autism: The International Journal of Research & Practice, 19*(2), 133–48. doi: 10.1177/1362361313517762

Centers for Disease Control and Prevention. (2012). *Facts about ASD.* Retrieved August 22, 2012, from http://www.cdc.gov/ncbddd/autism/facts.html.

Centers for Disease Control and Prevention. (2014). *Data & Statistics.* Retrieved April 26, 2014, from http://www.cdc.gov/ncbddd/autism/data.html.

Chiang, H., Cheung, Y., Hickson, L., Xiang, R., & Tsai, L. (2012). Predictive factors of participation in postsecondary education for high school leavers with autism. *Journal of Autism & Developmental Disorders, 42*(5), 685–96. doi:10.1007/s10803-011-1297-7

Ciccantelli, L. A. (2011). *Critical factors in successful navigation of higher education for students with Autism Spectrum Disorder: A qualitative case study.* Unpublished doctoral dissertation. University of Akron, Akron, OH.

Cohen, S. (2011). Providing services to students with Autism Spectrum Disorders. *Journal of Visual Impairment & Blindness, 105*(6), 325–29.

Deci, E. L., & Ryan, R. M. (1985). *Intrinsic motivation and self-determination in human behavior.* New York: Plenum.

Denney, S. C., & Daviso, A. W. (2012). Self-determination: A critical component of education. *American Secondary Education, 40*(2), 43–51.

Dente, C. L., & Coles, K. P. (2012). Ecological approaches to transition planning for students with autism and Asperger's Syndrome. *Children & Schools, 34*(1), 27–36. doi: 10.1093/cs/cdr002

Deris, A. R., & Di Carlo, C. F. (2013). Back to basics: Working with young children with autism in inclusive classrooms. *Support for Learning, 28*(2), 52–56. doi:10.1111/1467-9604.12018

Devlin, S., Healy, O., Leader, G., & Hughes, B. (2011). Comparison of behavioral intervention and sensory-integration therapy in the treatment of challenging behavior. *Journal of Autism & Developmental Disorders, 41*(10), 1303–20. doi: 10.1007/s10803-010-1149-x

Field, S. S., Martin, J., Miller, R., Ward, R. J., & Wehmeyer, M. L. (1998). Self-determination for persons with disabilities: A position statement of the Division on Career Development and Transition. *Career Development for Exceptional Individuals, 21*, 113–28.

Fombonne, E. (2003). Modern views of autism. *Canadian Journal of Psychiatry / La Revue Canadienne de Psychiatrie, 48*(8), 503–5.

Freedman, S. (2010). *Developing college skills in students with Autism and Asperger's Syndrome.* Philadelphia, PA: Jessica Kingsley Publishers.

Grandin, T. (2007). Autism from the inside. *Educational Leadership, 64*(5), 29–32.

Grzadzinski, R., Huerta, M., & Lord, C. (2013). DSM-5 and Autism Spectrum Disorders (ASDs): An opportunity for identifying ASD subtypes. *Molecular Autism, 4*(1), 1–6. doi:10.1186/2040-2392-4-12

Hagner, D., Kurtz, A., Cloutier, H., Arakelian, C., Brucker, D. L., & May, J. (2012). Outcomes of a family-centered transition process for students with Autism Spectrum Disorders. *Focus on Autism and Other Developmental Disabilities, 27*(1), 42–50.

Harpur, J., Lawlor, M., & Fitzgerald, M. (2004). *Succeeding in college with Asperger Syndrome: A student guide.* New York: Kingsley.

Hart, J. E., & Brehm, J. (2013). Promoting self-determination: A model for training elementary students to self-advocate for IEP accommodations. *Teaching Exceptional Children, 45*(5), 40–48.

Hendricks, D. R., & Wehman, P. (2009). Transition from school to adulthood for youth with Autism Spectrum Disorders: Review and recommendations. *Focus on Autism and Other Developmental Disabilities, 24*(2), 77–88. doi: 10.1177/1088357608329827

Hong, B., Haefner, L., & Slekar, T. (2011). Faculty attitudes and knowledge toward promoting self-determination and self-directed learning for college students with and without disabilities. *International Journal of Teaching and Learning in Higher Education, 23*(2), 175–85.

Hughes, J. L. (2009). Higher education and Asperger's syndrome. *Chronicle of Higher Education, 55*(40), 27–29.

Individuals with Disabilities Education Act Amendments of 2004, Public Law 105–117, 111 U.S.C.

Lane, J., & Kelly, R. (2012, April). *Autism and Asperger's Syndrome in the law student–making accommodations in academic assessments.* Paper or poster session presented at the 47th Annual Conference on (Re)assessing Legal Education, Oxford, UK.

Lyons, V., & Fitzgerald, M. (2007). Asperger (1906–1980) and Kanner (1894–1981), the two pioneers of autism. *Journal of Autism and Developmental Disorders*, *37*(10), 2022–23.

McDonough, J. T., & Revell, G. (2010). Accessing employment supports in the adult system for transitioning youth with Autism Spectrum Disorders. *Journal of Vocational Research*, *32*(2), 89–100. doi: 10.3233/JVR-2010-0498

National Longitudinal Transition Study-2. (2005). *The post-high school outcomes of youth with disabilities up to 4 years after high school.* Retrieved October 15, 2012, from http://www.nlts2.org/reports/2009_04/index.html.

Orsmond, G. I., Krauss, M. W., & Seltzer, M. M. (2004). Peer relationships and social and recreational activities among adolescents and adults with autism. *Journal of Autism and Developmental Disorders*, *34*(3), 245–56.

Pexman, P., Rostad, K., McMorris, C., Climie, E., Stowkowy, J., & Glenwright, M. (2011). Processing of ironic language in children with High-Functioning Autism Spectrum Disorder. *Journal of Autism & Developmental Disorders*, *41*(8), 1097–112.

Roberts, K. D. (2010). Topic areas to consider when planning transition from high school to postsecondary education for students with Autism Spectrum Disorders. *Focus on Autism and Other Developmental Disabilities*, *25*(3), 2022–23. doi:10.1007/s10803-007-0383-3

Roux, Anne M., Shattuck, Paul T., Rast, Jessica E., Rava, Julianna A., and Anderson, Kristy A. (2015). *National Autism Indicators Report: Transition into Young Adulthood.* Philadelphia, PA: Life Course Outcomes Research Program, A. J. Drexel Autism Institute, Drexel University.

S. Bill 1788, 82d Legislature §6 (2011)

Savoy, M. (2014). Autism: 5 misconceptions that can complicate care. *Journal of Family Practice*, *63*(6), 310–14.

Schlabach, T. L. (2008). *The college experience of students with Asperger's disorder: Perceptions of the students themselves and of college disability service providers who work with these students.* Doctoral dissertation. Retrieved from ProQuest. (3323938)

Schultz, S. M., Jacobs, G., & Schultz, J. (2013). A promising practice: Using Facebook as a communication and social networking tool. *Rural Special Education Quarterly*, *32*(4), 38–44.

Shankar, R., Smith, K., & Jalihal, V. (2013). Sensory processing in people with Asperger Syndrome. *Learning Disability Practice*, *16*(2), 22–27.

Shattuck, P. T., Narendorf, S. C., Cooper, B., Sterzing, P. R., Wagner, M., & Taylor, J. L. (2012). Postsecondary education and employment among youth with an Autism Spectrum Disorder. *Pediatrics*, *129*(6), 1042–49. doi: 10.1542/peds.2011-2864

Shattuck, P. T., Seltzer, M. M., Greenberg, J. S., Orsmond, G. I., Bolt, D., Kring, S., Lounds, J., & Lord, C. (2007). Change in autism symptoms and maladaptive behaviors in adolescents and adults with an Autism Spectrum Disorder. *Journal of Autism & Developmental Disorders*, *37*(9), 1735–47. doi: 10.1007/s10803-006-0307-7

Shogren, K. A., Wehmeyer, M. L., & Palmer, S. B. (2013). Exploring personal and environmental characteristics that predict self-determination. *Exceptionality*, *21*(3), 147–57.

Smith, C. (2007). Support services for students with Asperger's Syndrome in higher education. *College Student Journal*, *41*(3), 515–31.

Steere, D., & DiPipi-Hoy, C. (2013). Coordination in transition planning: The IEP/IPE interface. *Journal of Applied Rehabilitation Counseling*, *44*(1), 4–11.

Taylor, J. L., & Seltzer, M. M. (2011). Employment and post-secondary educational activities for young adults with Autism Spectrum Disorder during the transition to adulthood. *Journal of Autism & Developmental Disorders*, *41*(5), 566–74. http://dx.doi.org/10.1007/s10803-010-1070-3

Taylor, M. J. (2005). Teaching students with Autistic Spectrum Disorders in HE. *Education and Training*, *47*(7), 484–95.

Wolf, L. E., Brown, J. T., Bork, G. R., Volkmar, F. R., & Klin, A. (2009). *Students with Asperger Syndrome: A guide for college personnel*. Shawnee Mission, KS: Autism Asperger Publishing Company.

Zeedyk, S. M., Tipton, L. A., & Blacher, J. (2014). Educational supports for high functioning youth with ASD: The postsecondary pathway to college. *Focus on Autism and Other Developmental Disorders*, 1–12. doi: 10.1177/1088357614525435

Zylstra, R. G., Prater, C. D., Walthour, A. E., & Aponte, A. F. (2014). Autism: Why the rise in rates? *Journal of Family Practice, 63*(6), 316–20.

About the Authors

Emily Rutherford, EdD, received her Doctor of Education degree from Lamar University. She is currently assistant professor in the West College of Education at Midwestern State University. Dr. Rutherford has spent fourteen years working in public schools as a teacher, educational diagnostician, special education administrator, and as a university professor. Dr. Rutherford's experience also includes nearly a decade working as an evaluator and assessor for children suspected of having autism within a state agency. She presents at regional, state, and national conferences on autism, learning disabilities, and other related topics.

Jennifer T. Butcher, PhD, is an associate professor in the College of Education Center for Doctoral Studies in Educational Leadership at Lamar University. Dr. Butcher has more than thirty years of experience in the educational arena as a public school teacher, administrator, and university professor. She has presented at various international, national, regional, and state conferences. Dr. Butcher has published several journal articles and book chapters. Her areas of interest include special populations, college readiness, and student retention.

Lori S. Hepburn, EdD, is currently the ARD Facilitator/504 Coordinator at Nederland High School, and she also serves as the district transition designee in Nederland Independent School District. She is also an adjunct professor in the Center for Doctoral Studies in Educational Leadership at Lamar University. She has more than twelve years of experience in public schools where she has served in multiple capacities, including special education teacher, transition specialist, dyslexia specialist, behavior specialist, administrator, and college professor.